LANGUEDOC
& ROUSSILLON

THE HELM FRENCH REGIONAL GUIDES

Series Editor: **Arthur Eperon**

Auvergne and the Massif Central
Rex Grizell

The Dordogne and Lot
Arthur and Barbara Eperon

The Loire Valley
Arthur and Barbara Eperon

Provence and the Côte d'Azur
Roger Macdonald

LANGUEDOC & ROUSSILLON
Andrew Sanger

Photographs by Joe Cornish

CHRISTOPHER HELM
London

© 1989 Andrew Sanger

Photographs by Joe Cornish
Line illustrations by David Saunders
Maps by Oxford Cartographers

Christopher Helm (Publishers) Ltd,
Imperial House, 21-25 North Street,
Bromley, Kent BR1 1SD

ISBN 0-7470-3005-7

A CIP catalogue record for this book
is available from the British Library

Title illustration:
A chardon de soleil *nailed to a door,*
seen throughout the region (this one at la
Couvertoirade)

Typeset by Leaper and Gard, Bristol
Printed and bound in Italy

To *Gerry Dunham*
for her endless help, love and companionship

With thanks and affection ...

to Guy and Annie Gatty, at Montpellier;
Chantal Richard, at Aniane;
Mark Lintott and Judy Rothchild, of Octon;
Harold Chapman, of St. Guiraud (despite everything);
Simon Fairlie, who was the reason for going in the first place;
to David Barry (Baz), who cannot read this and whom we loved;
and all who connect me to this region of France.

Contents

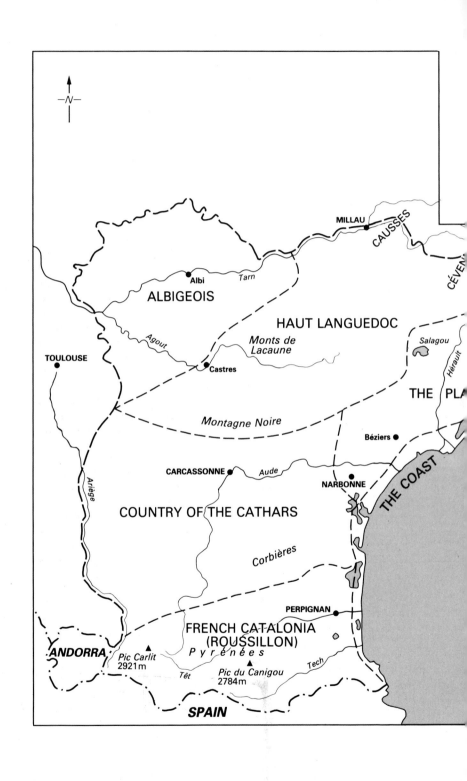

—N—

MILLAU
CAUSSES
CÉVEN

Albi
ALBIGEOIS
Tarn

HAUT LANGUEDOC

Agout
Monts de
Lacaune
Salagou

TOULOUSE
Hérault

Castres
THE PLA

Montagne Noire

Béziers

Ariège
CARCASSONNE
Aude

NARBONNE
THE COAST

COUNTRY OF THE CATHARS

Corbières

PERPIGNAN

ANDORRA
FRENCH CATALONIA
(ROUSSILLON)
Pyrénées
Pic Carlit
2921m
Têt
Pic du Canigou
2784m
Tech

SPAIN

1
Introduction

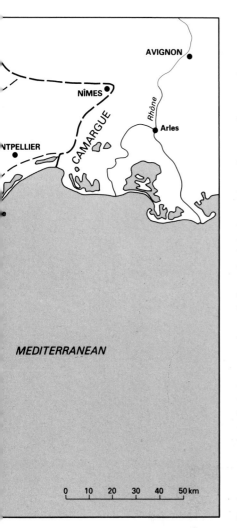

AVIGNON

NÎMES

Rhône

Arles

CAMARGUE

NTPELLIER

MEDITERRANEAN

0 10 20 30 40 50 km

Languedoc remains unknown, a mysterious name. Even the French hardly seem to know where it is, and those who do cannot pinpoint its borders. For connoisseurs of the French Mediterranean, Languedoc is the 'other' South of France; having come down the Rhône towards the southern sun, instead of turning left they turn right, into this region almost untouched by tourism, with lively towns nonchalant about their two and a half thousand years of civilisation, and a profoundly rural countryside seemingly silenced by the pressure of the sunlight, yet still echoing with the distant clamour of its eventful past.

For administrative reasons, the Government has joined Languedoc with its quite dissimilar neighbour Roussillon. Languedoc-Roussillon, as this twin creature has been officially named, conveniently combines a couple of remote and troublesome Mediterranean provinces, traditional enemies of Paris, both notoriously difficult to govern. Roussillon, a single département in the far south which was taken from Spain and added to France, remains culturally part of Catalonia. In Roussillon, though part of France since 1659, Catalan is still in everyday use, with French spoken by many only as a second language.

1

But for travellers Languedoc and Roussillon do indeed present an enticing unity. Its sandy coast extends in a single magnificent curve from the Camargue to the Spanish frontier. Inland, a sun-scoured plain backs onto unspoiled hills and mountains. Vineyards dominate huge stretches of the landscape: tens of thousands of higgledy-piggledy fields, oddly-shaped of differing sizes, climbing up stony hills in terraces or sprawling comfortably over the plain, but always with their vine-bushes arranged in neat orderly rows. They give way, with startling abruptness, to uncultivated country: occasionally to open heath and pasture, sometimes to forests of chestnut and beech and Mediterranean pine, but usually to the distinctive *garrigue*.

Garrigue is tough, resilient wild vegetation clinging tenaciously to rocky hillsides. It generally achieves little height, most of the plants being shrubs and bushes, but can form a ground cover almost impenetrably dense. Its spiky holm oak, prickly broom, thistly scrub, as well as fragrant multitudes of herbs — wild mints, strongly scented thyme, rosemary, wild lavenders and more — give the *garrigue* incomparable character, an intoxicating scent, a unique beauty.

Much of modern industrial development, to the chagrin of the central Government, seems to have passed the region by. Most of inland Languedoc remains incorrigibly rustic and rooted in the past. The locals themselves, whether sophisticates in Montpellier restaurants or habitués of down-to-earth village bars, seem affected by this sense of remoteness from the rest of the world and from the present-day.

Certainly, not to know where Languedoc's boundaries should be drawn is forgivable. For the name reveals nothing: *la langue d'oc* refers to a language rather than a place. Indeed, the name only began to be used in the 13th century, when much of the terrritory formerly claimed by the Counts of Toulouse came into the possession of the French Crown. 'Languedoc', to its new French administrators, vaguely denoted the part of the kingdom where French was not spoken. As centuries passed the Kingdom of France grew in power, embraced more regions, and consolidated its control over them. It was Napoleon who set about eliminating the cultural differences of all France's regions, and of course he had great success, hence the single French nation that we see today. But Languedoc's separate identity would not go away. The name Languedoc remained, its compass expanding and contracting, until it came to suggest, as it does now, all that coast, countryside and culture of the French Mediterranean west of the Rhône.

The language of the South, *langue d'oc* or Provençal, was one of the Romance languages — in other words it started life as Latin (the other Romance languages were Italian, Spanish, Catalan, French, Portuguese, Romanian and Swiss Romansch). It had many considerable differences from French, but also, as with all the Romance group, there were similarities. However, one of the differences was in the word for Yes. The Romans had no word for Yes; what they would say was Hoc Ille, meaning roughly (and a bit oddly to our ears), This That. In the southern language this became Oc. In the north of France it became O Il (or Oïl). So it was that the French coined the name *la langue d'oc* for the southern language, and *la langue d'oïl* for their own. At that time, languages did not really possess names other than being 'the language of such-and-such a place', and the name *langue d'oc* began firmly to indicate not only the tongue, but the place in which it was spoken. Meanwhile in the north of France the three main regional dialects of the *langue d'oïl*, Norman, Picard and Francien (or French), battled for a dominance which was eventually won by Francien — and the *langue d'oïl* gradually became known as French.

From the 11th to 13th centuries, the period of the troubadours, there was an unparalleled flowering of literature in Languedoc. Troubadours composed long lyric poems, *canso*, mainly concerned with courtly love, and travelled to the seigneurial courts of the South reciting their works. Their language was elaborate and elegant, and much imitated in Italy, northern France and Germany, where lyric poetry composed in the *langue d'oc* was almost as popular as it was in the South of France itself. After the Albigensian crusade, and the take-over of the South by the northern French, literature in the *langue d'oc* went into decline, although the language remained the normal speech of all southerners, with the usual dialect differences between one district and another. An edict of 1539 made the *langue d'oïl* the official language of the South, but not until the early 19th century, when it was legally prohibited to talk in the *langue d'oc* at school (a law repealed only in 1951), did the southern language really die out in everyday speech. Yet it does survive even now, as a *patois* (which is what its speakers actually call it) in the most

rural corners of inland Languedoc and the Cévennes. And of course the strong *accent du Midi*, the local accent with its distinctive sonorous tones, remains as a last inheritance of the old language of the South.

A sense of loss because of the destruction of Languedoc's culture and language has long affected southern artists, writers and intellectuals. As long ago as 1854, Frédéric Mistral's *Félibrige* movement attempted to revive Provençal as a medium for literature. Although the movement had little lasting impact on the arts, it did lead briefly to some good writing in the southern language, most of the best of it by Mistral himself. Frédéric Mistral was no doubt one of the influences which led to today's wider-ranging resurgence of a sense of separate identity in Languedoc. Study of the language, now more often known by the invented 19th-century name Occitan, has been encouraged by the Escola Occitana (founded 1919) and the Institut des Études Occitanes (founded 1945). Nowadays it is taught at Montpellier University and often seen in re-named street signs and regionalist graffiti. Occitan enthusiasts (while themselves sagely remaining Catholics) hold up the example of the Cathars and the Camisards as symbols of southern resistance, and they talk wistfully of a lost country called Occitania which they hope to restore — unaware perhaps that there never was any such place. This modern 'Occitan movement' represents rather confused longings for some degree of local autonomy (or even, at its most extreme wing, separate nationhood); a return to spoken *langue d'oc*; and a restoration of local traditions: all impossible, nostalgic dreams.

3

Languedoc's Climate

The plains of Languedoc and Roussillon have a typical Mediterranean climate with predictable seasonal weather. The long hot summers (July average 28°C) and short cooler winters (January average 12°C) are both dry seasons, with more rain falling in the brief spring and autumn. Although predominantly balmy, there can occasionally be strong winds and summer storms. The winds are known as the Mistral (very dry north wind from the Rhône Valley); the Tramontane (literally 'across the mountains', north-west wind carrying some cloud but usually not rain); and the Marin (moist hazy air from the Mediterranean, bringing rain). The rare east wind can bring more tempestuous weather. The Mistral when it blows gently in summer makes idyllic sunny days, but when it blows hard in winter brings low temperatures. According to local weather lore, the fine dry weather starts on 15th April and continues until 15th August, when there may be some storms; in mid-September there are many windy days; on 1st November the cooler dry weather of winter starts: February is the coldest month; and on 15th March rainy days herald the start of spring.

The inland hills have colder winters, with thick snow cover in the Pyrenees, but they benefit from exceptionally clear dry weather throughout the summer months.

Much of Languedoc's most fascinating 'sightseeing' is in the effects wrought by the work of nature rather than by the hand of man. The region's strange geology has created amazing phenomena. Even the Languedoc plain, on its relatively featureless journey round from the Rhône delta to the Pyrenean mountains, offers the curious *étangs*. These are low-lying, shallow lakes or lagoons filled with barely moving saltwater. This unusual environment used to attract mosquitoes, but they were eliminated in a huge programme during the 1960s; today the reedy waters are the haunt of astonishing flocks of elegant pink flamingos and other rare wading birds. Between these inland lakes and the sea extend thin strands, barely more than ribbons of sand, on which several coastal towns find enough space to live, enclosed by water.

Rising above these lowlands, the inland hills of the Haut Languedoc date from the earliest era of primeval rock formation. Their ancient crystalline granites and schists have been eroded by the passage of millennia, sometimes into remarkable, weird shapes; the *rocs tremblants* of the Sidobre, rocking stones delicately balanced one on the other, are one example of the form this can take. Fragments of rock more durable than their surroundings can be left protruding from a weatherworn landscape to create the most spectacular effects, such as at the chaotic Cirque de Mourèze, or the bizarre imitation 'townscapes' of *rochers ruiniformes*, ruin-like rocks, such as the group called Montpellier-le-Vieux.

Standing detached from the hills, lying between them, are the areas of high limestone plateaux called *causses*. Seemingly quite lacking in visual diversity themselves, the *causses* have created, with the help of thousands of years of rainfall, the most spectacular phenomena of all. The limestone plateaux are highly permeable: water falling on them simply disappears into the ground. Beneath the surface, it carves huge caverns or grottoes. Here rain drips down, bringing the rock minerals with it, to display an unearthly art of its own, stalactites and stalagmites, outlandish shapes, the water forever seeking a firmer base and, on finding it, turning into underground rivers and lakes. Many of these *grottes* are open to the public on guided tours. One such system of underground caves and tunnels has been put to excellent use for thousands of years — at Roquefort. Here, at the foot of the *causses*, vertical passageways in the cliffs allow air movement while keeping humidity and temperature constant; it was long ago discovered that this was the perfect environment for the growth of a certain bacteria which turns ordinary white ewes' cheese into the most delicious blue cheese in France!

The *causses* are sliced, as if they were themselves no more than slabs of cheese, by running water. Rivers, sometimes not especially wide, have cut steeply plunging canyons between one plateau and another. These gorges make dramatic scenery. High cliffs tower and overhang the narrow roads which try to follow the twisting rivers. The Gorges du Tarn, running north out of Languedoc into the Massif Central, is the best known — and deservedly so — of these extraordinary ravines. But there are several others: the Dourbie, the Jonte, the Vis. The twisting and turning of the rivers can be a strange sight in itself, as at the Cirque de Navacelles (which is what geographers call an 'incised meander'), on the river Vis, where the flowing water has cut right through a turn that became too convoluted.

Though not properly part of the Haut Languedoc region, the hinterland of the Aude and Ariège départements ('Land of the Cathars') is also hilly, and constitutes the foothills of the Pyrenees. Here too the landscape has been sculpted by long erosion. On either side of the valley of the Ariège deep caverns dig into the hills: in some, prehistoric Man has left drawings on the cave walls to remind us of his presence in this region. Inland from the Aude coast, the rugged Corbières, one of Languedoc's best wine districts, seems in parts almost a desert of picturesque wild rocks and barren peaks.

Ancient Languedoc was a melting-pot of the Classical world, absorbing Greeks, Levantines and Romans, who mixed with the native Iberian tribes. The first Greek settlements (Agde, Marseillan and others) were founded around six or seven centuries before Christ, and flourished by trading with other Greek towns around the Mediterranean. Romans made their first incursions into the territory in 118BC, conquered it with ease, and declared the whole area of what is now Languedoc and Provence to be a senatorial province, under the name Narbonensis, with its capital at Narbonne. The region was settled by Romans and traders from other parts of their empire, with many prosperous towns and cities both on the coastal plain and farther inland. In AD381, for simpler administration, the province was divided into Narbonensis Prima and Narbonensis Secunda, roughly equivalent to today's Languedoc and Provence.

Being so heavily Romanised, and very much part of the Mediterranean commerce not only in goods but in ideas, the region was Christianised in the earliest stages of the religion. When in AD313 Emperor Constantine (for political rather than religious reasons) decided to allow Christians the freedom to practise their faith, the offer was actively taken up in this part of his Empire. It was to remain for centuries a region intensely concerned with religious matters — and at times torn apart by doctrinal differences.

After the sudden Roman withdrawal in the 5th century, Visigoths from the north took over a large part of Languedoc, which they called Septimania. In the early 8th century, Moors (or 'Saracens') moved in from the south, but were driven back in 732 by Charles Martel, and forced to withdraw farther into Spain by Pepin 'le Bref' (the Short) in 759. Gradually a new feudal equilibrium emerged throughout Languedoc, with counts, viscounts and minor local lords, each vying to increase his power at the expense of the others. At the head of this framework, by the 10th century, stood the Counts of Toulouse. Their constant rivals for control of the area were the Catalan Counts of Barcelona and the Kings of Aragón, who possessed Roussillon and were keen to increase their possessions north of the Pyrenees. By the early 1200s, many important Languedoc towns had passed into their hands, including Montpellier, Millau, Béziers and Agde. Yet the reputation of the Counts of Toulouse and their territories as powerful, prosperous and cultured remained supreme.

These 10th, 11th and 12th centuries were important in the development of Languedoc's art and architecture. In both Languedoc and Roussillon, long exposure to Roman aesthetics, and an attraction to forceful simplicity rather than subtlety or delicacy of design, led to the building of many exceptional Romanesque churches and monastic buildings in this devout period. The most outstanding were in Roussillon, and St. Michel-de-Cuxa (10th and 11th centuries), St. Martin-du-Canigou (11th and 12th) and Serrabonne (11th and 12th), all in the Pyrenees, are still among the best examples from that era. There were many others though, still rewarding a visit today, for example at Fontfroide or St. Guilhem-le-Désert. The distinctive features of Romanesque building — the round arches, simple vaults, sturdy pillars, sombre but serene interiors — reflect not only the materials and methods of construction, but also a whole mentality. There is in these fine abbeys an underlying seriousness, a spiritual austerity and strength of purpose, which seems to guard itself against the sort of lightheartedness and artistic freedom which in other regions was to lead into the Gothic style.

Emanating mainly from Catalonia, via Roussillon into Languedoc, a 'Southern' style developed which was to retain many of its characteristics even when Gothic design did reach this area. A striking feature of this 'Southern' look is the absence of aisles: churches have a single broad nave, with perhaps side chapels to break the monotony. Another common sight in Languedoc, much rarer elsewhere, is the fortified church, protected against all sorts of menaces — Moorish invasions, gangs of brigands and, indeed, other Christians. Some of Languedoc's churches look more like fortresses than places of worship.

Defensive considerations were bound to be an important architectural influence in this troubled region. Hilltop castles and towns enclosed by massively impenetrable ramparts were everywhere in medieval Languedoc. The weak southern frontier needed strong fortifications, and every town large or small was constantly at risk from being involved in war. Local lords, whether in town or country, needed secure places of refuge in case their district came under attack. During the holocaust of the Albigensian war their castles all came into use, often to shelter Cathars from the onslaught. Many of these 'Cathar castles', although now largely reduced to ruins, remain as gaunt reminders of that vicious time.

Ultimately, Gothic building did reach Languedoc; at first it was deliberately and heavy-handedly imposed on the southern population after the end of the Albigensian Crusade (1229). The Church, after its victory over the heretical southern ideas, wanted to bring the latest architectural fashions from the orthodox North. These became coloured by much that was typically Languedocien. One of the best examples of this Southern Gothic style can be seen at Albi, in the immense brick cathedral. It is interesting to note, in the Albigeois, where building stone is lacking, that ordinary bricks proved highly effective in meeting the needs of both Romanesque and Gothic styles of architecture.

In the Middle Ages, Languedoc's trade with the rest of the Mediterranean world brought many Jews and Arabs, foreigners in strange dress who were tolerated here as nowhere else. Pilgrimages to the Holy Land were simpler from this starting point, and were undertaken more readily than by northerners. It was this cosmopolitan atmosphere, as much as the different language, which helped to make medieval Languedoc so different from the rest of France. The 'class' system, too, lacked the clear divisions typical elsewhere: a weak feudal structure, with too many impoverished nobles, allegiances which were never honoured, many freemen owing allegiance to no one, together with early urbanisation which allowed tradespeople to make fortunes greater than their lords, all contributed to making a society quite unlike the 'uncivilised' Franks to the north.

While nominally owing allegiance to the monarchs of both France and England, the Counts of Toulouse in fact retained complete independence. In the 12th century, their support for (or at least tolerance of) the Cathar 'heresy' which had swept Languedoc — Cathars held that there were two gods, one good and one evil — was the excuse needed by the King of France to invade and conquer Languedoc and bring it under his control. Added pressure was given by the imminence of a treaty between Toulouse and Aragón, which would make a united Catalonia and Languedoc far more powerful than France.

To put a stop to this, to enlarge his own kingdom, and to crush the southern religious heresy, in 1209 Philippe Auguste of France joined forces with Pope Innocent III to launch the Albigensian Crusade. In a bloody twenty years of savage warfare and slaughter the Crusade achieved all its objectives, effectively destroying Languedoc's culture and submitting the region to northern rule.

Yet that was not the end of Languedoc's rebelliousness. The rise of Protestantism provided the South with another opportunity to defy its northern conquerors. The new creed found enthusiastic support in Languedoc, and led to prolonged and furious violence during the religious wars of the 16th century. Many Languedoc towns were eventually given the freedom to practise their Protestantism under the Edict of Nantes (1598), but the revocation of the edict (in 1685) caused an outbreak of even greater violence against the Protestants, answered in kind by the fanatical Calvinist peasant guerrillas called Camisards. Based in the Cévennes, the Camisards received financial and moral support from all over Languedoc, but their Camisard War (1702–1704) proved a disaster for the region, ending in mass executions and the emigration of tens of thousands of its Protestants (although in many Languedoc towns and villages they are still numerous).

Predictably, growing Revolutionary feeling later in the 18th century gave yet another impetus to southern anti-establishment sentiments, but once again the 1789 Revolution and its subsequent rebellions led only to a more complete subjugation of Languedoc to Parisian control.

Yet even in the 20th century outbursts of regional passion have provoked serious uprisings against outside authority. Although conservative and tradition-loving, the peasantry of Languedoc is far from politically passive. In 1907 vine-growers rebelled against new laws permitting sugar and water to be added in wine-making and against imports of foreign wines, both of which were eroding farmers' incomes in the South. Calling their

cause, with a touch of melodrama, the Beggars' Revolt, over half a million vine-growers rioted in Montpellier. When local army units were called in, they would not take on the peasants. In the end, the farmers won the day and caused new regulations to be created to suit their needs. Something of the same mood was shown in the 1970s when Languedoc's wine-farmers felt threatened by foreign imports of wine. Roadsigns were painted out, highways closed, trucks overturned and their contents thrown away by local people determined to defend their region's livelihood. Again they succeeded. Even more recently the resolute, uncompromising and ultimately victorious movement to remove an unwanted expansion of an army base from the Larzac plateau has shown that Languedoc can still stand firm against outside rule. Sometimes, of course, this works in favour of Paris and the French, as during the Second World War when Languedoc provided the men and the morale for some of the most entrenched Resistance warfare against the Germans.

In the meantime, Roussillon, that fragment of Catalonia which lies north of the Pyrenees, had been constantly batted to and fro between various factions of French and Spanish rule. The driving out of the Moors in the 8th century left Catalonia as part of the County of Barcelona (until 1172), then the Kingdom of Aragón (until 1276). The creation of the Kingdom of Majorca, made up of all the Balearics and all Aragón's territories north of the Pyrenees, separated Roussillon from its fellow Catalans, but only until 1344, after which it was restored to them again within the reunited Aragón kingdom. In 1463, during a Catalan rebellion against Aragonese rule, Louis XI of France was able to seize Roussillon. But on the marriage of Ferdinand of Aragón with Isabella of Castile (1493), in a gesture of appeasement, and partly also because he was busy with wars on other frontiers, Charles VIII gave Roussillon back. This brought Catalonia under the control of Madrid, and was the start of the province's long struggle to be free of Spanish domination. While the rest of Catalonia fought for this goal right up until the death of Franco, Roussillon was liberated from Spanish rule several centuries sooner in a way that it had not expected. In 1659, in a remarkable piece of double-dealing with both Catalonia (which thought he wanted to absorb the whole province into France) and Spain (which simply wanted to weaken Catalonia), Louis XIII of France managed to recover Roussillon in the Treaty of the Pyrenees, which signed over everything north of the Pyrenees to him. Roussillon was allowed to keep its isolation, and France benefited from more defensible borders.

Roussillon has not proved as opposed to French rule as it was to Spanish. Links with the rest of Catalonia have increased in the last few years, but Roussillon — especially in the current climate of toleration for regional differences — seems content enough to form part of the diverse French nation. It produces, after all, a large proportion of the *vin de table* and fresh out-of-season fruit and vegetables which are so important to French life! In the modern age, despite (perhaps

even because of) the revival of interest in everything 'Occitan', Languedoc too has been more ready to accept that it truly is part of France, albeit with a strong regional accent. This has been helped by the setting up of the administrative region of Languedoc-Roussillon, which has taken some power away from Paris and given it to Montpellier. And in an effort to stimulate the region's languid economy, since the 1960s the Paris Government has spent vast sums to develop the Languedoc-Roussillon coastal resorts and bring both Languedoc and Roussillon into the mainstream of French life.

Museums and Galleries

Note that opening times of museums, etc. are liable to frequent alteration; many churches and religious buildings are closed between 12 and 2; churches should not be visited during services except to take part in the service.

Hotel and Restaurant Closed Periods

Note that most French hotels and restaurants close for 1 or 1½ days a week·(hotels remaining open only for guests already booked-in), and also may have longer closed periods of a week or a month. These dates may be varied from one year to the next.

Some French Words Used in the Text

Appellation or Appellation Contrôlée	highest official quality-control wine category
autoroute	motorway (usually with toll)
avenue, av	avenue
bastide	fortified medieval town on grid pattern
boules	French-style bowls, played on any open space
boulevard, bd	boulevard, avenue
causses	limestone plateaus
Cave, Cave Coopérative	winery owned communally by local wine-growers
CDT (Comité Départemental de Tourisme)	tourist office for the département
commune	administrative area like a ward or parish
corniches	high steep-sided bays descending to the sea
CRT (Comité Régional de Tourisme)	regional tourist office
département	administrative area similar to a county
esplanade	outdoor promenade, esplanade or terraces
Établissement Thermal	bath house or pump room at a spa
étang	shallow saltwater lagoon
garrigue	rough Mediterranean heathland
GR	Grande Randonnée — long-distance waymarked footpath
Logis, Logis de France	federation of family-run country hotels
OTSI	Office du Tourisme-Syndicat d'Initiative (see SI below)
paysan	local country person, usually a peasant farmer
place, pl	square
platanes	plane trees
préfecture	local administrative headquarters
quai	paved river embankment, often part of public highway
Relais et Châteaux	federation of independent luxury hotels of character
route de, rte de …	the road to …
route nationale	classification for a main road
rue	street, road
SI	Syndicat d'Initiative (local information office)
VDQS, Vin Délimité de Qualité Supérieur	official second-rank wine category
vieille ville	'old town', the historic quarter of a town
vignoble	vineyard region
Vin de Pays	'locality wine', lowest official wine category

10

Conversion Tables

km	miles	km	miles	km	miles
1	0.62	8	4.97	40	24.86
2	1.24	9	5.59	50	31.07
3	1.86	10	6.21	60	37.28
4	2.48	15	9.32	70	43.50
5	3.11	20	12.43	80	49.71
6	3.73	25	15.53	90	55.93
7	4.35	30	18.64	100	62.14

m	ft	m	ft	m	ft
100	328	600	1,968	1,500	4,921
200	656	700	2,296	2,000	6,562
300	984	800	2,625	2,500	8,202
400	1,313	900	2,953	3,000	9,842
500	1,640	1,000	3,281	3,500	11,483

ha	acres	ha	acres	ha	acres
1	2.5	10	25	100	247
2	5	25	62	150	370
5	12	50	124	200	494

kg	lbs	kg	lbs
1	2.2	6	13.2
2	4.4	7	15.4
3	6.6	8	17.6
4	8.8	9	19.8
5	11.0		

°C	°F	°C	°F	°C	°F
0	32	12	54	24	75
2	36	14	57	26	79
4	39	16	61	28	82
6	43	18	64	30	86
8	46	20	68	32	90
10	50	22	72	34	93

2
Food and Wine

Languedoc Gastronomy

Languedoc is a land of robust dishes with strong Mediterranean flavours, a vigorous aromatic cuisine, generous in olive oil, garlic and southern herbs. Juniper, sage, rosemary and, above all, thyme, which grow everywhere among the *garrigue*, are liberally used. Labourers working outdoors readily find other wild food to carry home for the evening table: snails (which thrive among the vines), leeks, *myrtilles* (bilberries, blueberries), cèpes mushrooms, sometimes even truffles among the roots of prickly holm oak, chestnuts in the hills and, of course, on days when they have come out armed with a shotgun, whatever hare or pigeon has been unfortunate enough to cross their path. Keen hunters like to meet for a Sunday morning outing to the woods to look for *sangliers*, wild boar, a dangerous catch.

A regional cuisine reflects other characteristics of the region. Languedoc makes no pretension to delicacy or refinement. This unyielding, sun-hardened land has given rise to a strong and sturdy people, hardworking and with hearty uncomplicated appetites. Thrift and self-sufficiency have governed the economics of the kitchen. Nevertheless, some of the traditional dishes of the region are quite demanding to prepare, and great pride and importance is attached to always using good-quality local produce.

Of course Languedoc's vine-cloaked plain, edged by the untameable vegetation of the *garrigue*, produces different ingredients from the green wooded inland hills, different again from the high plateaux at Languedoc's northern limit. Yet from the point of view of gastronomy, Languedoc is all one: it has a single character. Meat and cheese from the mountains are an essential part of the diet of people on the plain, just as fruit, vegetables and wines from the plain are considered 'local' in the hills. (Roussillon, however, the Catalan country down in the Pyrenees, is part of a quite separate tradition, and will be dealt with separately. Its all-year-round market gardens though are also vital to Languedoc's cuisine.)

Freshly killed wild game is highly favoured. In its simplest form, the meat, whether of *sanglier*, small birds, a whole goat, or shop-bought steak, is sprinkled with herbs and barbecued over the flames and in the smoke of *sarments*, vine cuttings. It's eaten with

Languedoc's Specialities

Aïgo bouïdo — *soup of garlic, herbs and bread, and often eggs (Albigeois)*

Aïllade — *garlic mayonnaise, aïoli*

Alicot, alicuit — *stew of goose or duck giblets, often with cèpes mushrooms (Albigeois)*

Bouillabaisse — *fish stew with scorpion fish (rascasse), conger eel (congre), and gurnard (grondin), among others, carefully seasoned with herbs, spices, a touch of orange peel and white wine (Coast)*

Bourride — *fish stew made of several firm white fish such as monkfish, turbot, etc., in a stock with herbs, spices, lemon peel and aïoli; served with bread and aïoli (Coast)*

Brandade de Morue — *a thick, creamy stew of pounded salt cod, garlic, milk and olive oil*

Cassoulet — *Languedoc's most famous dish, a very thick casserole made of white haricot beans, pork, sausages, goose fat, with plenty of garlic and herbs (recipes vary considerably:* Cassoulet de Carcassonne *contains lamb, which is expressly forbidden in the more traditional* Cassoulet de Castelnaudary)

Civet — *general name for a substantial stew of game cooked with onions, the animal's own blood and red wine; most popular is* civet de lièvre *(hare) and* civet de sanglier *(wild boar)*

Civet de Langouste — *crayfish stewed in white wine with onions, garlic and herbs*

Cousinat — *a thick stew of chestnuts cooked with cream, and sometimes with other fruits (Haut Languedoc)*

Daube — *slow-cooked meat casserole or stew*

Estofinado — *dried cod dish with potatoes, eggs, nut oil and milk*

Estouffade — *may refer loosely to any stew, but especially of white haricots, pork, garlic and tomatoes*

Fèche Sec — *salted dried pig's liver served with radishes*

Flaunes — *light pastry with goats' cheese*

Gâtis — *a pastry or brioche with cheese, often Roquefort*

Gras Double — *popular tripe stew with ham, garlic, vegetables and herbs*

Grattons — *fried pork crackling with pieces of bacon*

Marrons glacés — *the luxury end of chestnut dishes, candied chestnuts*

Marron purée — *chestnut paste, used in several dishes*

Ouillade — *succulent traditional stew of cabbage and beans, first cooked separately then mixed*

Oulade — *stew of cabbage and other vegetables with pork and sausages*

Pignons — *pine kernels, used in omelettes and other dishes*

Rouzolle — *highly seasoned chopped meat, as stuffing or on its own*

Saupiquet — *piquant, salty sauce, usually with cream, wine vinegar and juniper berries, popular with game, especially rabbit*

Trénouls, trénels — *sheeps' tripe stuffed with ham, garlic, herbs, sometimes vegetables, and sometimes eggs (Causses)*

bread and salad, and plenty of strong red wine. Called a *méchoui* in these parts, the barbecue has a popular place not just in local cooking but in a festive bringing together of friends and family in the balmy air of a southern night. It makes a popular summer dinner in Languedoc.

This is also a region of charcuterie, terrines, preserved pork meats and sausages of assorted shapes and sizes. The Montagne Noire, on the southern limits of Haut Languedoc, produces excellent hams, and strong-flavoured charcuterie brought down from the high Roussillon is everywhere available. Black and white puddings, offal and tripe continue to be especially popular in the small mountain towns and villages of both Languedoc and Roussillon. Foie gras, turkey and goose pâtés, and *confits* (the meat of a fowl cooked in its own fat), made in the hill districts, are much used everywhere.

Among the most abundant and most liked of all meats is the herb-fed lamb or mutton from the hills and plateaux of Haut Languedoc. Often, mutton or beef — not always tender in this area — are prepared *en daube*, that is, cooked long and slow in a rich stew.

Indeed stews or casseroles are the most typical dishes of Languedoc. Undoubtedly the best known of them all is the solidly filling cassoulet. Originally from Castelnaudary, which still claims to know more about it and make it better than anywhere else, cassoulet has become almost a hallmark of Languedoc gastronomy. Politicians can win votes by saying they like it, or lose them by being seen not to. To describe it merely as a bean-and-pork stew (which it is) ignores not only the complexity of the preparation, which

can take a full day and requires bacon rind, pork fat, goose *confit*, knuckle of pork, loin of pork and pork sausage, but also the endless debate about the proportions of the ingredients, and whether or not a cassoulet which contains lamb is worthy of the name!

Another great Languedoc stew is the full-flavoured fish soup, *brandade de morue*, made mainly of salted cod. In past centuries this preserved fish provided a reliable standby for nourishment when other staple crops proved capricious. The fish is pounded to a creamy consistency and cooked with generous amounts of garlic in milk and olive oil. But apart from this traditional favourite, despite the long coastline and despite Sète's importance as a fishing port, seawater fish is surprisingly not much eaten in Languedoc. Towns close to the sea are an exception, with menus featuring other fish stews, notably *bouillabaisse* and *bourride*. Only on the coast itself, particularly in the town of Sète, are sea fish eaten fresh.

By contrast, the inland rivers, cool, clean and broad, produce plenty of superb freshwater fish, especially trout, which is much liked, well-prepared, and makes a frequent appearance on restaurant menus. Shellfish, too, oysters and mussels produced in huge quantities in the coastal *étangs*, are a popular choice throughout Languedoc, though obviously more so near the sea than in the remote interior.

Languedoc's principal cooking oils are olive and grape seed, used for almost everything (luckily both are highly nutritious and cholesterol-free). However, for certain dishes, especially in the hill districts, pork and goose fat are important too. Cassoulet, for example, depends upon a liberal use of pork fat. Dried beans are nearly always prepared with pork lard, but oil is used for cooking other vegetables.

Irrigated and highly productive vegetable gardens and fruit orchards (especially in the Roussillon river valleys) make a great contribution to Languedoc's cookery. Huge, succulent, juicy tomatoes are extremely abundant, and are beyond compare with any that are grown farther north. A tomato 'salad' — a simple plate of sliced tomato sprinkled with herbs — makes one of the most delicious starters imaginable. Freshly picked, and amply sized, aubergines (eggplants) with their dark purple skin, large green peppers with a sheen of freshness, and firm courgettes (zucchini) (often still with their edible yellow flower attached) are in generous supply at all the markets, alongside the piles of onion and garlic and several varieties of crisp *salade*, lettuce. There are even one or two entirely vegetable dishes, most notably *ratatouille*, the famous southern stew of aubergines, courgettes, peppers, onions and tomatoes, all cooked (separately at first, then mixed) in olive oil with plenty of garlic and thyme.

Chestnuts grow in profligate quantities over large areas of the inland hills. To a considerable extent they remain ungathered, perhaps for the reason that not so very long ago they provided the staple food of the poorest of country people. Nevertheless, chestnuts do still find their way into many a dish in the hilly regions. They may be served as a vegetable, as a stuffing, or in the form of *cousinat*, a creamy chestnut stew.

As for the cheese course, taken as a whole Languedoc can hardly be counted as a great cheese-making region. Yet it does produce France's King of Cheeses, the delicious, piquant, creamy blue Roquefort, made by maturing ewes' milk cheese in the caves at Roquefort-sur-Soulzon, a village in the shadow of the Causse du Larzac. Roquefort, besides being sometimes the most enjoyable part of a meal when served on the cheeseboard, allows adventurous chefs some flights of creativity when using it as an ingredient in other dishes. For example, a light pastry filled with Roquefort may well be offered as a starter or side dish. Small goats' milk cheeses — pelardon, picardon and others — are widely sold at markets by small farmers. Because the pasture tends not to be sufficiently lush, cows are not much seen in Languedoc, other than in the Monts de Lacaune. But a certain amount of cows' milk cheese does get made, for example Passé l'An, firm, strong-flavoured, and coated with oil, and Bleu des Causses, similar to Roquefort but less subtly piquant and creamy than the ewes' milk version.

In keeping with the tradition of simple peasant cooking using local produce, the favourite desserts are fruit *tartes* (flans) making good use of whatever happens to be in season. Suddenly when the peaches are ripe, for instance, they are available everywhere in all the markets at astonishingly low prices. Likewise apples, eating grapes, cherries. Especially common, and absolutely delicious when cooked, are *myrtilles* (bilberries, blueberries). Another dessert well-made here, widely available from pâtissiers and often served as a restaurant dessert, is fresh ice cream.

In addition, and possibly even more distinctive of this part of France, the pâtissiers in towns large and small make not just the usual French-style pastry, but local speciality cakes and pastries: very sweet, usually with a biscuity or nougaty texture, they are often heavily flavoured with almond, pistachios or oranges.

Roussillon-Catalan Gastronomy

Languedoc and Roussillon, in food as in almost everything else, follow somewhat different traditions, although they also have great similarities. As in Languedoc, Roussillon's cooked dishes use plenty of olive oil, garlic and herbs. One curiosity of the region is that bitter oranges are sometimes put into savoury dishes. Vegetables are even more abundant here, sweet peppers being among the most freely used. Anything hunted or gathered from the wild is, even more than in Languedoc, a cornerstone of local cooking, and especially popular in the mountains — boar, deer, rabbit and other game and birds, fish from the rivers, wild fruits from the woods and meadows, and particularly the many sorts of mushrooms which flourish here.

Above all, the great speciality of the region is charcuterie: dried sausages, local kinds of 'salami', hams (*jambon cerdan*), black pudding and white pudding, and preserved meats generally. Among the most popular are preserved pork sausages Baton de Berger, Fouet, Llangounisse, Ronyonal; blood puddings called Bottifarra; and Pa de Fetge (literally, liver bread), a

rich, substantial pork 'sausage' with added eggs, garlic, parsley and pepper; as well as all sorts of pâtés, some mixed with wild mushrooms.

Roussillon is not a dairy region. The cattle one sees are being reared for meat, and few cheeses are made apart from Pyrénées, a mild cows' milk cheese with a thin black rind, and small rounds of strong goats' cheese. But when it comes to confectionery, there is no lack. Among the distinctive Arabic-style sweet specialities of the towns and villages are various small sugar-coated cakes and biscuits with plenty of honey, aniseed, almonds or orange-blossom: rousquilles, tourons catalans, bunyelles, tourteaux à l'anis ... especially delicious are local panallets, little marzipan sweets with nuts.

Wines

Every mealtime in both Languedoc and Roussillon is preceded by its apéritif, usually *pastis* (anis-flavoured spirit diluted with cold water; not made locally), and accompanied by a bottle or carafe of local wine.

At the risk of seeming dismissive, perhaps it is excusable to admit that the greatest merits of Languedoc's wine are that there is plenty of it and it is cheap. Over half of France's *vin ordinaire*, oceans of which daily wash down relaxed, comfortable dinners in homes and restaurants all over the country, comes from Languedoc's immense plain, where vines are a virtual monoculture. And half of France's VDQS wines (*Vin Délimité de Qualité Supérieure*, the category below *Appellation Contrôlée*) come from Languedoc. So too does a large proportion of the EEC's undrinkable

Roussillon–Catalan Specialities

All y oli — *aïoli, garlic mayónnaise*

Anchoïade or Pa y all — *anchovy and garlic paste*

Barboufat or Brou Bufat — *a clear meat soup, by-product of sausage-making*

Boles de Picoulat — *meatballs (beef and pork mixed) in sauce*

Boulinade or Bullinade — *a stew of sea fish, including scorpion fish, gurnard, whiting and monkfish, cooked with onions, garlic, peppers and potatoes*

Cargolade — *literally just means snails; a favourite Catalan picnic dish, snails 'barbecued' on a fire of vine cuttings, and served with charcuterie, slices of lamb, bread spread with garlic mayonnaise, and local red wine*

Friand de Fromage — *puff pastry filled with hot (usually goats') cheese*

Moulade — *grilled moules, mussels*

Mouton à la Catalane — *mutton cooked in white wine with ham, garlic and vegetables*

Oulade — *a popular stew eaten at home: pork, sausage, beef, cabbage, potatoes, white beans and other vegetables*

Perdreau à la Catalane — *very popular stew of partridge, peppers and bitter oranges*

Salade Biquetoux — *'biquetoux' is a type of goats' cheese, in this case served with a mixed salad*

Saucisse à la Catalane — *slices of spicy sausage fried with herbs, garlic and orange peel*

Trinxat — *cabbage, potatoes and ham dish*

'wine lake'. Government efforts to persuade *viticulteurs*, vine-growers, to switch to other produce such as asparagus have met with little success in this tradition-bound region. A better scheme, meeting with a more positive response, is to encourage a change to grape varieties from which superior wines can be made. Recently some of the best *VDQS* have earned an upgrading to *Appellation Contrôlée*, and some of the bottom rank have found themselves elevated to *Vin de Pays* status (the category below *VDQS*).

The *Vin de Pays* classification was introduced in 1973 to indicate which were the best of the previously ungraded local wines, and there are now over 130 of them nationwide. Of these, over 60 come from Languedoc (and five from Roussillon). Vin de Pays d'Oc is one of them, and is drawn from the whole region; others include Vin de Pays de l'Aude and Vin de Pays de l'Hèrault. Many are from small, or even tiny, wine-making districts which deserve to be singled out. Among them are, for example, the de Cassan, des Coteaux Cathares, des Coteaux de la Cité de Carcassonne, des Coteaux de

Narbonne, des Coteaux du Salagou, de Cucugnan, des Gorges de l'Héraut, de Pézenas ... there are many more, and it is worth experimenting, since some are good and all are inexpensive.

For all that, most Languedoc wines are unpretentious reds, palatable enough but undistinguished. They are a perfectly satisfactory accompaniment to everyday meals. Almost all are produced by co-operatives of vine-growers from neighbouring villages and are made in communally-owned *Caves Coopératives*. The best of them are entitled to be called by the vague *Appellation* Coteaux du Languedoc. One can usually stop by at a village *Cave Coopérative* for a taste of the local vintage and a bottle or two at rock-bottom prices. If you take a container, it can often be filled unceremoniously at an even lower price.

A few places on the plain now (quite justifiably) pique themselves on being well above the average; they have worked hard to improve their wines: for example, the districts of Montpeyroux and St Saturnin, on the slopes at the edge of the Languedoc plain, or St Georges-d'Orques, west of Montpellier, St Chinian and Faugères near Béziers, and Narbonne's two vineyard areas La Clape and Quatourze. At the *Cave* in these villages, one is expected to take the *dégustation* (tasting) a little more seriously — and pay a little more! (Note though that not *all* the village wines entitled to use the Coteaux du Languedoc label — there are thirteen altogether — are as good.) Not many rosé or white wines are made on the plain; the best of them is the *Appellation Contrôlée* dry white Clairette du Languedoc.

Interestingly, for much of their red wines, Coteaux du Languedoc producers use a very short maceration period, just one night (hence St. Saturnin's name 'Vin d'Une Nuit'). As a result the colour is oddly light. Vin Gris, 'grey wine', is another variation: a light pink, made by pressing red grapes before fermentation begins. All Coteaux du Languedoc rosés, whites and light reds should be drunk young and cool, while only the few darker reds may age well for a couple of years and should be drunk, as is more usual with red wine, at around 16°C.

Up in the Albigeois, along the banks of the Tarn, in a district with Gaillac at its centre, the vineyards produce a wine under the general Côtes du Tarn label. Again, these are mostly red, enjoyable and very adequate for everyday drinking, even if not deserving of much contemplation. In a smaller part of the area, still with Gaillac at its centre, some of the more superior wines qualify for the Gaillac appellation. But even of these it is only the slightly *pétillant* white Gaillac Perlé which stands out, although a few of the reds are making great improvement. Oddly enough, the price gives nothing away here: all Côte du Tarn and Gaillac reds, whites and rosés are astonishingly cheap, indeed a bargain; but they are often all marked at the same price, whether on supermarket shelves or restaurant wine lists, despite the fact that the Perlé is usually strikingly better than the others. It is almost invariably on offer in the restaurants of the Albigeois, and sometimes in other parts of Languedoc too, and can be one of the best dry white wines in this region.

The rocky Corbières (lying mostly within the Aude département) produces enjoyable strong dark red wines in huge quantities. Slightly better are those from the Minervois, on the borderline between Corbières and the Montagne Noire. Both Corbières and Minervois have now gained *Appellation Contrôlée* status. Best of all the Corbières reds is from the little patch (actually two little patches) called Fitou, which has long enjoyed a well-deserved *Appellation Contrôlée* designation. Don't drink it young — it benefits from being kept for a few years. There remains one other Corbières district to mention: the white wines of Limoux. Ordinary dry white Limoux, quite palatable, is called Vin de Blanquette. Much more interesting is its sparkling white called Blanquette de Limoux, reputedly one of the first sparkling wines ever developed (10th century). Now using the *méthode champenoise* with great success, sparkling Blanquette is crisp, fresh, enjoyable. It's very inexpensive, and comes dry, medium or sweet.

Fortified sweet wine made from the muscat grape, known as Vin Doux Naturel, is the most surprising of all Languedoc wines. Chilled, it makes an excellent apéritif, with a strength and richness reminiscent of sweet sherry, and with a powerful muscat flavour. Vins Doux Naturels come only from a few places, notably Lunel and Mireval, near Montpellier; Frontignan, next to Sète; and most of all from the Roussillon coast and plain.

Despite the name, there's nothing especially *naturel* about these muscat wines, except that they are sweetened by adding proper wine alcohol, not sugar. By contrast, Languedoc is a leader in the development of a type of wine which is much more 'natural' than that — *vin biologique*, or organic wine. These vary enormously in quality, since all they have in common is that no chemicals are used in growing or making the wine. Some have been highly praised, for example Mas de Daumas Gassac, from a small vineyard near Aniane. Its production is low — say one glass of wine per square metre of vineyard — but three-quarters of the grapes used are of the Cabernet Sauvignon variety, a finer grape than is usually grown in this region. For me, *vins biologiques* are indistinguishable from any other wine, although one cannot doubt that from a health consideration it must be better not to have all those pesticides and preservatives swimming about in one's drink.

Roussillon too produces delicious sweet muscat wines and large quantities of robust reds. In general, Roussillon offers a better (not wider) selection than Languedoc. As well as the unpretentious, very drinkable, inexpensive *Appellation Contrôlée* reds (three areas: Le Collioure, Côtes du Roussillon and Côtes du Roussillon-Villages), and the robust, good-value *Vins de Pays* classification (five sorts: des Pyrénées-Orientales, Vin de Pays Catalans, des Côtes Catalan, des Coteaux de Fenouillèdes and des Vals d'Agly), Roussillon produces top quality sweet wines, fortified wines, and powerful, strong-flavoured apéritifs, liqueurs and digestifs. 95 per cent of France's Vins Doux Naturels of *Appellation Contrôlée* standard come from Roussillon, the best of them from Banyuls, Maury and (particularly good) Rivesaltes. Of the stronger drinks, the most famous of Roussillon's local apéritifs is one which is something of an acquired taste, Byrrh, made in the distilleries at Thuir, near Perpignan.

3
The Albigeois

The Albigeois is where ancient sun-baked Languedoc pushes north-west to meet the green mountain slopes of the Massif Central and the richer pastures of the old provinces of Péri-gord and Quercy (today's Dordogne region). Its capital is the big, industrious town of **Albi** (pop: 48,300), which rises from both banks of the broad river Tarn. The old heart of the town lies on the south side, while later districts extend north of the river.

See old Albi from across the Tarn in the evening sunlight, with swallows flying and whistling over the swirling water. Beside the river rise the mass and might of Albi cathedral and its epis-copal palace, their brickwork seeming draped in red by warm southern light. The Roman-tile rooftops of the old town, too, heaped and huddled chaot-ically one beside another, have a ruddy, earthy, smouldering colour, and the uneven brick arches of the Pont Vieux, built in 1035 (altered since), still stride across the river towards the 'red town'.

Of course, Albi is called the red town only because it is made all of red brick — of a hue and shape rather different from what we are used to. But red brings to mind too the violent history of this rebellious city. Indeed, it gave its name to one of the bloodiest of

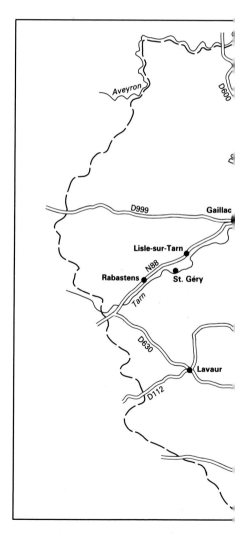

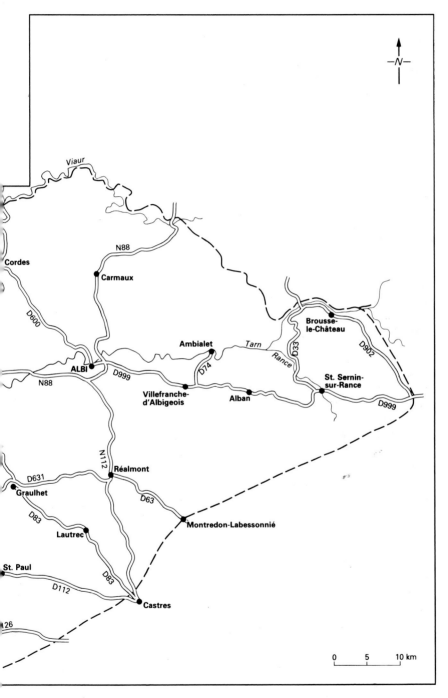

Viaur

Cordes

N88

Carmaux

D600

Brousse-
le-Château

Ambialet

Tarn

D33

D902

ALBI

D999

D74

Rance

St. Sernin-
sur-Rance

N88

Villefranche-
d'Albigeois

Alban

D999

N112

Réalmont

D631

Graulhet

D63

D83

Lautrec

Montredon-Labessonnié

St. Paul

D83

D112

Castres

26

0   5   10 km

religious civil wars — the Albigensian Crusade, when the Papal armies under northern leadership swept into the South determined to conquer and destroy. Their mission was to wipe out the Cathar heresy, which had taken root in all the villages and towns of the diocese of Albi. The Pope pardoned in advance all sins committed during the Crusade's first forty days, while the King of France gave an undertaking to the knights and barons who led the army that any lands they seized would become their own. In fact, Albi by no means suffered the worst of it: many other communities were virtually wiped out, their citizens — Catholic and Cathar alike — systematically slaughtered. (More about Cathars, and what they believed, on p. 109).

After the Albigensian conquest, many new cathedrals were built in Languedoc. Massive, powerful, usually fortified, they were meant to cow the defeated population, and demonstrate the invincible might of the Church and of the North. Albi cathedral is one of the most extraordinary examples of that mood.

If nothing else, the monumental cathedral which dominates the city of Albi is an astonishing feat of brick-laying! But as a work of art it is vile. Indeed, it was never intended as a work of art at all. Built in the wake of the Albigensian conquest, it ˙ was intended only to awe, to subdue, to silence the defeated citizens. It looks like a fortress, forbidding and relent-less. Yet walk up the grand staircase and through the massive porch — an incongruously ornate later addition (of pale stone, not brick) — into the cool

Albi, viewed from across the river Tarn

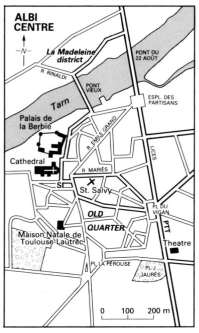

ALBI
CENTRE

La Madeleine
district

PONT DU
22 AOÛT

R RINALDI

PONT
VIEUX

Tarn

ESPL. DES
PARTISANS

Palais de
la Berbié

R. EMILE GRAND

LICES

Cathedral

R MARIÈS

St. Salvy

PL DU
VIGAN

PTT

OLD

QUARTER

Maison Natale de
Toulouse-Lautrec

Theatre

PL LA PÉROUSE

PL J.
JAURÈS

0   100   200 m

Town plan A

interior of the building, and you discover a different world, curiously small and more intimate (considering how big the place looks from outside), and fantastically highly decorated with hardly a centimetre of wall space unadorned. The message for all medieval dissenters evidently was — if you are outside the Church you will be confronted only with brute force; if you are inside, a believer, we offer this heavenly beauty, gold and glory.

And while the cathedral's exterior is simple and austere, much of the interior decoration is in the most lavish Gothic style. The choir screen especially, added in the 15th century (like the equally elaborate porch), is Flamboyant Gothic at its most exuberant — but astonishingly delicate, like finest lace. The choir is huge, taking up much of the interior space; notice the choir-

stalls, which are magnificently carved. Turn round from the choir to face the western wall: seen from here the great organ, built by Moucherel during the 18th century, is impressive. Beneath the organ, the wall is covered with a huge fresco of the Last Judgement, and beside the organ loft, a staircase winds up to the top of the belltower, giving a superb view across rooftops and river into the green countryside beyond. Hardly had the organ been installed than anti-religious Revolutionaries smashed up and removed much of the cathedral's ornamentation and statuary. Nevertheless plenty remains, including the martyred Sainte Cécile, to whom the cathedral is dedicated, lying elegantly on her side after being struck with the axe.

After the Treaty of Meaux in 1229 which formally ended the Albigensian Crusade — though the hunt for southern heretics went on well into the 14th century — Bernard de Combret, the newly appointed bishop of Albi, set to work constructing a heavily fortified palace where he could live relatively unaffected by the hostility of the local people outside his walls. After him came the notoriously tyrannical bishop Bernard de Castanet who, in 1282, took in hand the building of the well-defended cathedral.

Bernard de Combret's episcopal palace, still standing in its handsome gardens beside the cathedral, is known locally as le Palais de la Berbie. This curious name (for berbie means nothing in French) is thought to come perhaps from the Occitan word besbia, bishop. Although outwardly a stern and defensive building, inside it is palatial enough, with beautiful parquet floors, embroidery-draped walls and highly decorated ceilings. The gardens, on a

A Chronology of the Albigensians

Mid-12th century: Cathar ideas find growing support throughout Languedoc, especially the diocese of Albi.

1176: At Lombers (16km from Albi) church authorities publicly question local Cathars about their beliefs; the churchmen condemn the Cathars as heretics.

1181: At Lavaur (48km from Albi), military force is first used against Cathars.

1198: Pope Innocent III vows to eradicate Catharism. At first he sends envoys and preachers throughout Languedoc to try to dissuade its supporters.

1208: Papal envoy Pierre de Castelnau is assassinated at St. Gilles (near Nîmes) as he tries to persuade Cathars to return to the Catholic Church. The Count of Toulouse is accused of complicity in the crime and is excommunicated.

1209: The Pope and King Philippe Auguste of France jointly organise the Albigensian Crusade.

1209–1229: The Crusade terrorises southern Languedoc, slaughtering tens of thousands of people and putting numerous towns and villages to the torch.

1229: The Treaty of Meaux ends the Crusade; the whole of Languedoc is placed under the authority of the French Crown.

1229–1300: French troops continue to search out Cathar strongholds and destroy them. An Inquisition, based at Carcassonne, is used to determine who is a Cathar and impose suitable punishments.

1244: Fall of Montségur, symbol of Cathar resistance, after a final 9-month siege.

1255: Fall of Quéribus, last of the Cathar strongholds.

1300s: Catharism reappears among the peasantry in the mountainous Comté de Foix district (Aude and Ariège départements). The Inquisition is used with severity to arrest, question and execute or punish whole populations of villagers in the area, effectively completing the last eradication of Catharism.

(See also: p. 109).

high terrace overlooking the river Tarn, though rather formal, are shady and tranquil, and make a pleasant stroll.

Today a large part of the Palais de la Berbie is devoted to Albi's most illustrious son, and one who could not be more out of keeping with a bishop's residence — Henri de Toulouse-Lautrec (1864–1901). His pictures, well displayed in chronological order, show his development over the years from a youth tied to his mother's apron strings to a rather depraved adult observer of the seediest side of Parisian low-life. It's touching to see that in the midst of his Parisian period he made occasional visits back home and again painted his sad and disappointed, but

Albi: backstreet in the old town

still devoted mother. Although the subjects are often more than slightly erotic — with titles like 'Woman pulling up her stockings' or 'Woman on all fours' — it is clear that Toulouse-Lautrec, embittered perhaps by the childhood accidents which left him crippled and dwarfish all his life, saw the ugliness in things as well as the beauty. In one room, some of the palace's original portraits of po-faced bishops and church dignitaries have remained fixed to the walls, and now look down with false righteousness on a collection of Toulouse-Lautrec's famous posters!

In all the main boulevards and central squares there can be quite a lot of traffic, but step into Albi's tangled network of old lanes and narrow winding streets, which extend from the modern central square, place du Vigan, down to the cathedral, and suddenly there is peace.

This area, 'le Vieil Alby', has been largely cleaned up and made into a smart shopping district; yet there is still plenty to discover here and it rewards a little exploratory walk. Most of the grander old buildings, like the Palais de Justice and the Hôtel de Ville, are made all of red brick. But a few of the very oldest houses stand out with their picturesque timbers. Hidden away behind the houses and shops — and reached down tiny alleys, each going into a different street — the lovely Église Saint-Salvy has calm, restful cloisters dating from the 11th century. Cross rue de Verduse into what is now called rue de Toulouse-Lautrec and find, at number 14, the artist's birthplace, the *Hôtel du Bosc*, a large attractive substantial old house covered in virginia creeper.

Here the young Henri had his two accidents, which left him crippled and deformed for the rest of his life, and here he spent the years of his privileged yet tragic childhood, often travelling out to visit his mother's family home in the countryside at Celeyran. Today the house has become a museum of the artist's life, revealing something of the day-to-day existence of a 19th-century aristocratic family, and during the summer months with exhibitions of paintings and drawings (sometimes on loan from abroad) illustrating themes from Toulouse-Lautrec's works.

A man whose name has been commemorated in the names of *rues* and *places* in almost every city in France is the dynamic socialist politician Jean Jaurès (1859–1914). In fact he was born at nearby Castres (see p. 44), but lived at Albi, where he was a lecturer in philosophy at the *lycée* for many years before going into politics. One of his several attempts to encourage socialism in action was to persuade (and finance) striking glassworkers to set up their own Verrerie Ouvrière, Workers' Glassworks, which is still one of Albi's most important industries and, indeed, still under communal ownership.

Albi today is a busy, lively, important local centre, certainly not much scarred by the sad events of the past. Indeed, in the usual French way, they have been turned into a spectacular Son et Lumière, held on summer evenings, which tells the story of the Albigensian Crusade with all the pageantry that the citizens can muster! Open-air markets are held in place Jean-Jaurès, but the real life of the town revolves around the adjacent place du Vigan. A busy boulevard, called *les Lices*, runs down from here to the new Tarn bridge, named pont du 22–août (commemorating Albi's liberation from German occupation in 1944). The bridge, and the luxurious Altea Hotel at the far end of it, give an excellent view back across the river to the cathedral and old town.

In all the best pâtisseries of Albi, incidentally, you will find the ring-shaped, aniseed-flavoured little cakes called gimblettes and petits jeannots. Charcuteries stock the region's numerous savoury pork and sausage specialities, like frittons, bougnettes, melsat,

The secretive little cloister of St. Salvy, Albi

27

Henri de Toulouse-Lautrec

The son of Count Alphonse de Toulouse-Lautrec Montfa and Adèle Tapié de Celeyran (who were cousins), Henri was born on 24th November 1864 at the Hôtel du Bosc, a mansion belonging to his father's family since the 17th century. He was artistic from the first, painting and sketching members of his family and riding scenes at Celeyran, his mother's family home.

In 1878, the young adolescent Henri fell from a chair in one of the lounges in the house and injured his legs; a similar accident the following year compounded the damage and his legs failed to grow after that age, leaving him disabled and dwarfish.

In 1882, leaving home, Toulouse-Lautrec moved to Montmartre in Paris, then a seedy and bohemian quarter. He painted numerous scenes from revues, cabarets and brothels and other entertainments, particularly capturing the combination of the enticing and seductive settings with the tragic quality of the performers themselves. He was no mere disinterested observer, however, himself leading a totally depraved and sensual life. Even at this stage he returned occasionally to Albi and Celeyran, and curiously on these visits would paint his old subjects — especially portraits of his mother.

To earn more money, from the late 1880s he took to poster design and made a huge success in this field; his advertisements for revues and shows are probably the most famous of his works. Alcoholism and ill-health caused him to retire to a clinic at Neuilly in 1899, although, after a course of treatment which seems to have been successful, he rapidly returned to his habitual way of life. In 1901, his health in a much worse state than before, he left Paris and went to 'recover' at another of the Toulouse-Lautrec family's residences, the château of Malromé (Gironde); he died there on 9th September that year.

and others. And on every restaurant wine list, the cheapest *Appellations* on offer are the local Côtes du Tarn and, better, the reds and whites from nearby Gaillac, an astonishingly good, bargain-priced wine little-known outside this area.

The Côte du Tarn district encompasses quite a large area, including Albi itself, but the vineyards of Gaillac lie to the west of the town, farther down the Tarn on the way to Toulouse, another 'Red City' (in more ways than one), and former capital of the Counts of Languedoc. Indeed all the towns along the flat road (N88) from Albi to Toulouse are made of the same distinctive rosy coloured brick.

An interesting alternative route, at least at the start of the journey, is to leave Albi on the Cordes road, turning left after about 4km onto the little country road (D1 — slightly hidden by a bend in the road) to **Castelnau-de-Lévis**. This small, well-placed village preserves the ruins of its feudal fortress, including a tall, narrow tower with a remarkably fine view over the countryside and the city of Albi. Carry on along the minor roads to Marssac, where the *route nationale* to Gaillac can be picked up.

Why Red Bricks?

France is exceptionally well endowed with building stone, and every region has developed architectural styles reflecting the kinds of stone most readily available. Visitors travelling across the country see everywhere stone mansions and stone cottages. Only two parts of France are lacking suitable stone for building: Flanders in the extreme north, and the southern Midi Toulousain basin between Auch and Albi. The traditional answer to the problem was brick. In the Toulouse and Albi region, the manufacture of bricks, tiles and cement from local materials is now an important industry. Bricks have been made in the area for many centuries — as can be seen from the medieval architecture of the Albigeois.

The bricks of Albi and Toulouse do not resemble modern bricks, but follow in their Roman tradition. Roman bricks were thin and square, about 5cm thick, and anything from 20 to 61cm wide (modern bricks are $7.5 \times 10 \times 23$cm). Medieval bricks — like those used to build Albi Cathedral — were similar, often about $5 \times 25 \times 33$cm. The texture was more 'clayey' than hard modern bricks, and colours softer and less uniform, with some redder, some yellower, some browner than others, giving to the buildings of Albi and its neighbours their distinctive warmth and character.

Despite the wine, **Gaillac** itself is of really only minor interest, with its crumbling modern brick buildings and rather characterless main squares, place de la Libération and place de Hautpoul (which comes to life on market days), and the N88 pounding through the town. And although thriving as the commercial centre of the region's wine trade, Gaillac is not even within the white wine area which has made its name! Apart from a small labyrinth of narrow streets clustered around the fortified tower of Saint Pierre church, hardly anything remains of Gaillac's older nucleus. The original main square of old Gaillac was the little place Thiers, with its sunken fountain, arcaded sidewalk and old houses. A walk through this quarter quickly reaches the Tarn and the riverside abbey church of Saint Michel, with its very plain red brick Romanesque style

enhanced only by a fortified tower. For the best view of the church, and the town, see it from the pont Saint Michel over the Tarn.

By contrast, the next town along the road is much more enjoyable. While its name, **Lisle-sur-Tarn**, obviously suggests a river island (*l'isle*, the island), in fact it is a 12th- and 13th-century *bastide* standing securely on the river's right bank. *Bastides*, fortified medieval 'new towns', were characterised by arcaded main squares, and at Lisle the square remains beautifully preserved, a lovely sight with its timbered brick houses and shops. Leading off the square, though, the 13th-century dwellings look crumbling and seedy, though fascinating. Along narrow back lanes some overhanging houses almost touch — in fact, some have actually been joined up. Notice that many of the old houses alternate brick with

rounded stones taken from the river-bed. The 13th-century brick church near the river has survived in excellent condition. The town is enclosed by fertile, productive fields, including vineyards cultivated for over a thousand years.

Take the riverside minor road which passes through the village of **Saint-Géry**. Surprising in such a simple and rustic setting, here stands the impressive château where Richelieu stayed when visiting the area in 1629. Two sphinxes, stern and exotic, guard a fine entrance courtyard. The most recent parts of the building are late 18th century, but the East Wing, the kitchens and oratory date from the 14th. The most remarkable feature of the place though, is the splendid quality and quantity of furnishing which has survived — something quite unusual in French châteaux, which tend to have been stripped during the Revolution. It is only open to visitors on afternoons during July and August; the rest of the year it is closed except for Sundays and holidays.

Continuing along the Tarn, the narrow backroads pass between flat fields and vineyards to rejoin the fast N88, which soon reaches **Rabastens**. Or you could stay on the country lanes by taking D13, through Loupiac on the Tarn's south bank, and cross the river to enter the agreeable little town of Rabastens. From the high bridge, the brick ramparts of the town can be seen, but one cannot appreciate the age and appearance of the old bridge itself except by descending to the waterside.

The medieval city of Cordes clustered on its hilltop

The fortified tower of the church of Notre Dame du Bourg dominates the town. This building, like every other in these parts, is made of pale narrow red bricks; but the interior, with a single nave and side chapels in the Southern Gothic style, is plastered and intriguingly painted with fading frescoes and strange signs and crests. Notice too the curious esoteric symbols on the porch pillars — these are the insignia of the Guilds of the craftsmen who built the place. The Mairie, in the attractive main esplanade beside the route nationale, also has an unusual brick tower and here another odd piece of heraldic symbolism can be seen: the town crest, showing the Fleur de Lis, the Languedoc Cross, and three turnips! Why turnips I don't know, for Rabastens is a wine town, part of the Gaillac district — and the local produce bought direct from the *Cave Coopérative* is particularly drinkable. There's a pleasant little hotel at Rabastens, Le Pré Vert: near the central esplanade, it has a pleasant shady courtyard-garden, and a good unpretentious restaurant.

Not all the Albigeois is redbrick country. Away from the flat landscapes, anywhere where there are hills, the more familiar stone cottages reappear, clustered together in every village. At Gaillac, a turn onto the unfrequented D922, towards Cordes, leads at once into delightful rolling countryside. From the pretty village of **Cahuzac-sur-Vère**, in the midst of this lovely rustic scenery, D1 leads away west along the pleasing Vère valley.

Stay on D922 to reach **Cordes**. If instead you drive here direct from Albi, the road runs along a high ridge with fine views across the plains and vineyards of Gaillac. Perhaps the best approach of all into Cordes is from the north, coming from the spectacular countryside around Laguépie and Najac and the river Aveyron. But from any direction the town rises surprisingly and suddenly before you, mirage-like on its perfect hilltop.

All roads arrive at the bottom of the hill, and it is possible either to walk or to drive to the top. Driving is obviously quicker and easier, but walking up the narrow, cobbled lanes — though horrendously steep — is more in keeping with the character of the place, and gives a clear impression of the strategic sense of the location, as well as a good chance to admire dozens of gorgeous flower-covered (many climbing roses) mansions and cottages. Near the top of the hill, gates lead into the old heart of the town. Grand rue de l'Horloge is a pedestrian street leading all the way up.

Established in 1222, and named for the Spanish city of Córdoba, the original town was a walled *bastide*, standing right on the summit of the hill and enclosed within a triple line of ramparts. Modern visitors may wonder what attracted people to live in such an inaccessible spot: the great advantage of it was religious freedom. Cordes was founded by Raymond VII of Toulouse as a refuge and fortress for the local people who, although by this time the Albigensian Crusaders had already ridden through most of the region enforcing the Catholic orthodoxy, still remained incorrigibly dissident. Several years after the Treaty of Meaux declared the Crusade over, Church Inquisitors came to Cordes to investigate the rumours that many of the population were still Cathars. The rumours were true — and the Inquisitors were lynched. French troops who

then came to deal with the town took one look at the place and, so the story has it, simply turned around and rode off without even attempting to attack it.

This no doubt explains why in the hundred years which followed, many of Languedoc's surviving gentry — landless in the wake of the anti-Cathar confiscations — moved to Cordes and constructed magnificent mansions within the walled town. Several of these remain in quite astonishingly good condition ... Maison Prunet, Maison du Grand Veneur, the splendid Maison du Grand Ecuyer, covered in greenery and now an excellent hotel, and many more. The Maison du Grand Fauconnier, one of the finest of them, now houses the Mairie and Syndicat d'Initiative. In later centuries, narrow winding cobbled streets and steps, lined with simple stone cottages which today look unbelievably picturesque, cautiously crept out of the town walls and down the hillside. A gradual economic decline left Cordes rather neglected and forgotten by the 19th century, when fortunately Viollet-le-Duc, that ubiquitous architect of the Historical Monuments Department, ordered the restoration of many of the finer buildings. Its revival was boosted in 1940 by the moving in of a whimsical group of artists, oversentimentally calling themselves L'Académie de Cordes-sur-Ciel, which in turn attracted other painters and art-lovers.

As always with the medieval *bastide* town plan, the main square is a spacious arcaded marketplace. Today the covered market — les Halles — in the middle of the big square serves as a shady, pleasant area for café tables and outdoor *rendezvous*. Young and old alike gather here to talk or sit, enjoying the balmy air and sociable atmosphere.

Main Albigeois Festivals and Events

July

Theatre Festival, Albi — *first half of the month, invited theatre companies perform in the town*
Fête du Grand Fauconnier, Cordes — *colourful 12th-14th July medieval costume festival*

July and August

Music Festival, Cordes — *officially lasts from June to September, but most concerts are in July and August; lots of different kinds of music*
Music Festival, Albi — *classical music performances in the cathedral and Palais de la Berbie*

August

Amateur Cinema Festival, Albi — *showing of short amateur films in 9.5mm format*

September

Automobile Grand Prix, Albi

The weekly produce market is still held here every Saturday. Cordes, it must be admitted, has acquired a little too much of the 'arty' quality, and has a few too many tourists: but that is not always a disadvantage. It gives a certain bohemian *joie de vivre*, and attracts traditional entertainers like the young man who, during our visit, stood in the main square and, in a strong voice, to the accompaniment of a curious miniature barrel organ, sang favourite old French songs for a few *sous*.

The ancient 91m-deep well in the marketplace deserves a peer down. It is remarkable not only for its depth but also its 2.7m diameter, cut down straight through the rock. For a franc you can have the benefit of illumination to see the water far below. The water level, interestingly, always stays

the same depth, 12m. The legend is that those unwelcome Papal Inquisitors who paid a visit to the town ended their days by being thrown down this well, but clearly that doesn't make any sense at all. It is unthinkable that the townsfolk would so poison their own water supply. The more likely truth is that the story was invented as anti-Cathar propaganda.

While in Cordes, try a 'Navette Cordaise', speciality of local pâtissiers; it's a buttery plain cake (trapezoid shape) with almonds on top, and goes well with a tea or coffee. And if you're in the area at around the time of the July national holiday, note that Cordes' Fête du Grand Fauconnier (12th–14th July) is a popular lively festival at which everyone wears medieval costume. If you haven't anything medieval in your

33

suitcase, don't despair — appropriate attire can be rented for the occasion.

From Albi the main road, N112, plunges towards the south across flat farmland. A worthwhile stop along the way is **Réalmont**, a small riverside *bastide* built in 1270. Its pleasant main square, and agreeable atmosphere and location, have made it a popular stop-over for visitors passing through this area. Nearby there are a number of medieval churches and châteaux of note. Some 15km south-east, for example, is **Montredon-Labessonié**, within the Parc Régional du Haut Languedoc, with a ruined 12th-century castle; close by stands the Château de Castlefranc; while 10km to the south-west of Réalmont is charming **Lautrec**, handsomely placed on the slopes of a hill with some good views. Once a powerfully fortified little *bastide*, Lautrec still preserves the arcades of its main square, as well as part of the old ramparts and the Porte de la Caussade, last survivor of the original eight gateways into the town. It still has a good deal of charm and atmosphere, especially on market day (Friday morning). When browsing in town and village markets in this district, always look out for top quality garlic to take home, for it is cultivated just here. There is even a fair of *l'ail rose* in Lavaur each August. The *rose*, pink garlic, is stronger, but more importantly, keeps longer, than the *blanc*, white garlic. (The garlic season runs from July to April.)

Lavaur, reached either from Gaillac or Réalmont, has attractive old quarters beside the river Agout and a brick cathedral built in 1254 to replace an earlier building destroyed by the Albigensian Crusaders. Lavaur was an early stronghold of Catharism. In 1211 its fortress was besieged by the Crusaders, but put up strong resistance under the leadership of the châtelaine, Lady Geralda. When Lavaur was finally taken, she was thrown into a pit and buried alive with stones, her knights were hanged, and, in the words of one of the Crusaders, 'Our pilgrims also burned innumerable heretics with great rejoicing'. The 'innumerable' unrepentant heretics — actually about 400 people — were gathered in a field outside the walls and burned alive in a single huge fire.

East of the fast N112 on its plain, and east from Albi, lies a very different sort of countryside, of high green hills, unsophisticated villages, a rustic and sparsely populated terrain belonging in spirit partly to the Massif Central as well as to Languedoc.

From this magnificent landscape flows the Tarn, marking perhaps the boundary of these deep allegiances. This part of the river is little known to tourists, who are far more interested in the famous Gorges du Tarn section much farther east. That stretch of river is certainly more dramatic, as well as more crowded, yet somehow the Gorges drive is less satisfying than discovering that even when the Tarn leaves its ravine the broad river is as stately and beautiful as ever, the valley still imposing and majestic.

The most attractive route, to follow the Tarn upstream from Albi, is along the south bank. For a superb one- or two-day tour through this part of Languedoc's backcountry, first set off from Albi (take rue de la République, which is the N99, signposted Millau

Refreshing shade at Cordes

Bastides

Bastides were the new towns of their day, built to a straightforward grid plan of principal streets (*carreyous*) and connecting alleys (*androns*), with a spacious central market square with arcaded sidewalks (*cornières*) and a fortified church. Defensive ramparts and fortified gates kept out unwanted visitors. Nowadays they tend to attract rather than repel visitors, for those which have managed to retain their original features, especially the arcaded main square, have tremendous appeal and charm to the modern eye. However, functional rather than aesthetic considerations were behind the founding of these sturdy medieval walled towns. Almost all of them were built in the areas most affected by the violence and factionalism of the protracted dispute (12th-15th centuries, especially the Hundred Years War, 1337-1453) between France and England over the title to Aquitaine and the rest of western France (for in 1152 almost one-third of the country had passed into the hands of the English Crown). Both the English and the French nobility constructed *bastides*, along identical plans, where their subjects could live in relative safety and freedom, in order to reinforce their hold over the disputed territories. The area of *bastides* reaches over from the Atlantic coast well into western Languedoc, with good examples in the Albigeois at, for instance, Lisle-sur-Tarn, Cordes and Réalmont.

and St. Affrique, through Albi's eastern suburbs, then take the left fork D100 to St. Juéry. From here simply follow the riverside road, which starts unremarkably but soon improves. In places the river winds about crazily, and the road skips from one meander to the next.

Ambialet, on first arrival, is a puzzling spot. It seems hard to work out exactly where this uncentred little village stands — on which side of the river. In fact it lies squeezed between the two sides of the Tarn's most convoluted meander of all. Just here, the broad river turns back on itself so sharply as to create a most peculiar 'peninsula': at one point the river flowing east is just 23m from the same river flowing west. A narrow rocky ridge, pierced by a road, separates the two. (And the weird concrete 'château' at

the neck of the peninsula is a hydro-electric power station.) The village itself is nothing special, but the site is startling. For an excellent view of it, which explains everything, on reaching Ambialet follow signs to the 11th-century Benedictine Priory at the summit of the ridge. Quite apart from its overview of the local geography, the priory church Notre-Dame de l'Oder does deserve a visit. Inside it is small, beautiful, simple, sombre.

Ambialet attracts a surprising number of day-trippers, but stay with the river as it continues into yet more pleasing and unfrequented country. Cross to the north bank at Villeneuve to see the small spa village of **Trébas**. Trébas claims — how plausibly I don't know — that its natural springs, which rise at a constant 16°C, are the most copper-rich mineral waters anywhere in Europe. To this sceptical English traveller, that doesn't sound particularly healthy! Each village along the way has a rustic traditional appearance, the cottages all of unfaced stone. Follow the road on this side of the river as far as, say, tiny **Lincou** with its riverside church with grey slate steeple. Both sides of the Tarn are very pretty at this stage. Pass through the rustic hamlet of **St. Dalmazy** (or Dalmazi) with its small parish church, and, at the confluence of the little Alrance and the wide Tarn, reach the village of **Brousse-le-Château**.

Although every other place along the way has been quite picturesque, Brousse comes as a surprise. A fortified walled village rising on the steep narrow ledge between the two rivers, Brousse is rustic and dark, with greenery clambering up to the cottages from the bank of the Alrance. As the main road rushes by on one side of the little river, a lovely old cobbled footbridge crosses over into the narrow unpaved lanes of the village. These alleys are too narrow for vehicles, and too steep, and the place retains a marvellous quality of being quite unable to fit the basic dimensions of 20th-century life. There's a fortified church where Compostela pilgrims used to stop, and at the summit of the hill stands the ruined fortress which gave the village its name. In fact, though, Brousse-le-Château has not been altogether by-passed by time, for it has been largely restored and does attract a few cognoscenti. There's even a nice little 1-star Logis at the riverside here, where you can have a good, remarkably inexpensive 4-course dinner, and spend the night.

The old footbridge and castle at the village of Brousse-le-Château

The Tarn valley road, sometimes rising high for a plunging overview of the landscape, sometimes clinging to the water's edge and criss-crossing the river on narrow bridges, continues its spectacular journey through tiny farm villages and small country towns towards Millau (see p. 57). To explore the magnificent unvisited Albigeois countryside south of the Tarn, turn back from Brousse-le-Château and follow the signs to St. Sernin. The road follows a very pretty route through wooded hills and between tranquil farms. It reaches **Plaisance**, a village above the river Rance, crowned by a handsome Romanesque former Benedictine abbey church with an octagonal tower, and continues along the Rance into **St. Sernin-sur-Rance**. The houses which line the narrow medieval streets of this provincial town seem anxious, like human beings, to conceal their age. For behind the bland modern façades are stone dwellings many centuries old. Some of the most striking, revealed to the eye, are truly grand mansions with fine exteriors and doorways. The Mairie (town hall) is a good example. St. Sernin's 15th-century church, with its hall-like Southern Gothic interior of single nave and side chapels, is attractive and its two carved wooden galleries are unusual.

The roads west towards Alban are high up, running across hill meadows and green fields in pleasing countryside with a clean, fresh feeling. **Alban** itself, a busy little agricultural centre, has a few unexpected works of medieval art — 16th-century gilded wooden Virgin and Child, Romanesque holy water stoop, 16th-century calvary — in its parish church. The road north from here to Ambialet on the Tarn is especially attractive, on a lofty ridge with views on both sides, while several picturesque routes lead farther west from Alban, through the fortified *bastide* **Villefranche-d'Albigeois**, built in 1239, continuing either towards the city of Albi or south into the *Monts* of the Haut Languedoc region.

Hotels and Restaurants

ALBAN: Hôtel-Restaurant au Bon Accueil (63.55.81.03), pleasant, comfortable 2-star Logis de France.

ALBI: Altea Hôtel, 41 rue Porta, by pont 22-août (63.47.66.66), has top-class food and accommodation and the best views in Albi.
Hôtel-Restaurant le Cecilia (63.56.61.11), first-class restaurant and just 4 bedrooms, surprisingly located in leisure complex with pool, tennis, etc.
Mapotel and Hostellerie St. Antoine, 17 rue St-Antoine (63.54.04.04), excellent restaurant and member of good, comfortable hotel chain.
Hôtel-Restaurant Modern' Pujol, 22 av du Colonel-Teyssier (63.54.02.92), 3-star Logis de France, central position, good restaurant.

BROUSSE-LE-CHÂTEAU: Relays du Chasteau (65.99.40.15), modest village hotel and restaurant, charming and very inexpensive.

CORDES: Hôtel-Restaurant du Grand Ecuyer, rue Voltaire (63.56.01.03), outstanding hotel and restaurant in one of Cordes' finest old mansions.
Hostellerie du Parc (63.56.02.59), 2-star Logis de France hotel with good restaurant.
Hôtel-Restaurant Vieux Cordes (63.56.00.12), reasonably priced, comfortable 2-star Logis.

FONVIALANE (3km north-west from Albi): **La Réserve**, rte de Cordes (63.60.79.79), beautifully situated quiet hotel with excellent restaurant.

MARSSAC (10km west from Albi): **Restaurant Francis Cardaillac**, on N88 (63.55.41.90), highly acclaimed.

RABASTENS: Hostellerie du Pré-Vert, 54 Promenade des Lices (63.33.70.51), charming Logis de France hotel with good restaurant.

RÉALMONT: Hôtel-Restaurant Noël, 1 rue de l'Hôtel-de-Ville (63.55.52.80), attractively located 2-star Logis hotel (also with apartments) and excellent restaurant.

ST. SERNIN-SUR-RANCE: Hôtel-Restaurant Carayon, pl du Fort (65.99.60.26), marvellous old Logis de France hotel with excellent low-priced restaurant, also with apartments.

Hotel Bookings Service

Loisire-Accueil: TARN — Hôtel du Département, Albi (63.54.65.25).

Museums

ALBI: Maison Natale de Henri de Toulouse-Lautrec: 14 rue Toulouse-Lautrec, Albi (63.54.21.81). The handsome house in which Toulouse-Lautrec was born and spent his childhood. *Open 1st Jul–31st Aug daily 9.30–12, 3–7.*
Maison du Vieil Alby: corner rue Puech-Béranger/rue de la Croix Blanche. *Enquire at tourist office.*
Musée Toulouse-Lautrec: in the Palais de la Berbie, episcopal palace, beside the cathedral. Very extensive collection of works from all periods of the artist's life. *Easter–1st Oct open daily 9–12, 2–6; 1st Oct–Easter open daily (exc Tue) 10–12, 2–5. Closed 1st Jan, 1st May, 1st Nov, 25th Dec.*

AMBIALET: Musée: inside Priory. Collection of objects brought from Brazil by missionaries. *10–12, 3–6.*

CORDES: Musée Charles Portal: by Porte de Rous. History of Cordes. *1st Apr–1st Nov: 9–12, 2–6; 2nd Nov–31st Mar: Sun 2–6 only.*
Musée Yves Brayer: inside Maison du Grand Fauconnier (SI). Art gallery. *1st Apr–1st Dec: 9–12, 2–6 (exc. Sun and fêtes, 2–7pm only); 2nd Dec–31st Mar: 9–12, 2–6 by request at the Mairie.*

GAILLAC: Musée d'Histoire Naturelle: pl Philadelphe Thomas (63.57.36.31). Natural history collection. *Visits by request.*
Parc de Foucaud, and 17th-century *château*: outside town on Graulhet road. Terraced riverside gardens by Le Nôtre *always open.* Art and history museum in château, *open Apr–Oct: 3–5pm daily (exc Tues); Nov–Mar: 3–5pm Weds and Suns only.*
Pierre de Brens Mansion. 15th-century mansion with museum of wine and local customs. *Apply to SI for visit (4pm only, Tues–Sat).*

LAUTREC: Musée d'Archéologie: in the Mairie. Local finds. *Sun 2.30–6pm summer only.*

LISLE-SUR-TARN :Musée Raymond Lafage. Local art and history. *Sun 11–12am only.*

ST GÉRY Le château (63.33.70.43). *Open Easter to 1st Nov: Sun and fêtes, 2–6 pm; except Jul & Aug, when open daily 2–6pm.*

Tourist Offices

CRT offices (regional information): 12 rue Salammbô, 31200 Toulouse (61.47.11.12).
CDT offices (information on the département): TARN — Hôtel du Département, Albi (63.54.65.25).
OTSI offices (local information): ALBI — pl Ste-Cécile (63.54.22.30); CORDES — Maison du Grand Fauconnier (63.56.00.52), summer only; GAILLAC — pl de la Libération (63.57.14.65); RABASTENS — 6 pl St-Michel, summer only.

Where there is no tourist office, apply to the Town Hall (Mairie or Hôtel de Ville).

4
Haut Languedoc

The Inland Hills

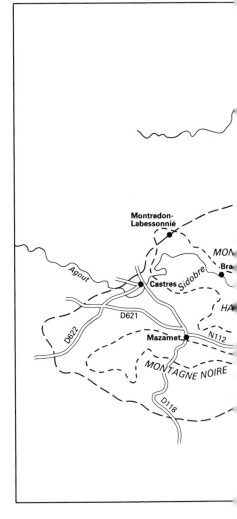

Right across the middle of Languedoc is a little-known, unvisited land. It comes as a surprise to discover just how much of this Mediterranean province is in fact balmy, temperate, wooded hill country. From the Montagne Noire to the plateau of Larzac, from Castres to Bédarieux, there's hardly a vine in sight, but instead a dense cover of greenery and wild flowers, of chestnut and beech forest, which has nothing in common with the more familiar Languedoc of plain and coast. This is the Haut (literally, High) Languedoc: these uplands are really the last southern limits of the Massif Central. Geologically complicated, Languedoc's ranges are formed of the most ancient of granite rock over which, in places, millions of years of erosion have scattered 'debris' of massive boulders, worked into some astonishing rock formations, while farther north the high *causses*, great limestone plateaus as permeable as sponges, are riddled with underground hollows carved out by the falling of water, and sliced by the deep ravines of flowing rivers. In cleared open country, high meadows nourish huge flocks of sheep kept for their milk; the farms are simple, the people traditional, and the villages muddily old-fashioned and rustic.

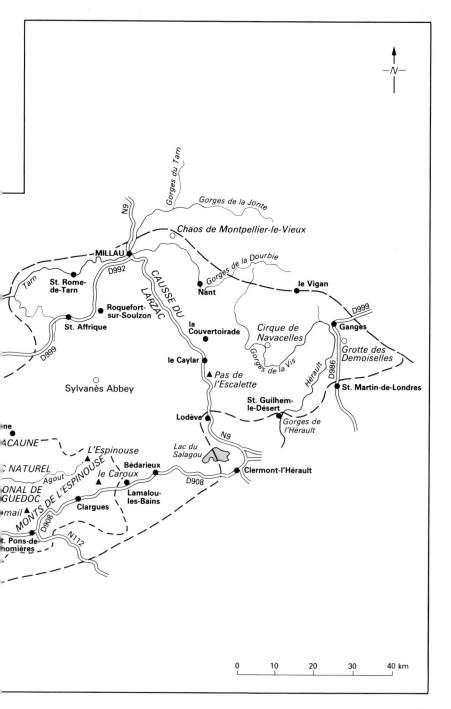

Haut Languedoc's small backroads offer numerous superb drives, and walks too. For the discerning map-reader, the whole area is dotted with little things to see which invite a pause: modest Roman remains, caves and grottoes, rivers and lakes. Much of the southern part of the area is contained within the Parc Naturel Régional du Haut Languedoc, the 'Regional Nature Park'. **Castres** (pop. 47,000), a big industrial town in flat country, might seem an improbable place to start exploring the Haut Languedoc, but in fact it makes an excellent entry point into one of the most interesting parts of the Regional Park. Clearly of Roman origin (*castrum*, a camp), Castres today is a busy, modern workaday place, with a refreshing attitude to tourism. It

makes absolutely nothing of its attractions. Along the embankments of the river Agout which flows through the town, old houses with balconies overhang the murky water. Sharing a building with the Hôtel de Ville is the Musée Goya, with a small collection of his work, mainly excellent portraits of ghastly looking aristocrats, and paintings by a number of other (mainly Spanish) artists. The Hôtel de Ville of 1669, with Le Nôtre's immaculate formal gardens behind, was originaly the Bishops' Palace; the 17th-century cathedral, with its Baroque interior, stands opposite. Also inside the Hôtel de Ville there is a museum devoted to the town's most illustrious son, the 19th-century socialist politician Jean Jaurès, whose name (though not,

Jean Jaurès

Few towns in France have not commemorated this socialist politician in the name of some *place* or *boulevard*. Born at Castres on 3rd September 1859, Jean Jaurès went to the school, in town, which has also been renamed in his honour. On finishing his education, he left Castres to take up work as a teacher of philosophy at Albi and then at Toulouse. He became an ardent and eloquent socialist at this stage in his life, and while in Albi helped striking glassworkers to start their own factory — the Verrerie Ouvrière, Workers' Glassworks — which is still communally owned by its employees. Entering politics, he was elected as a socialist *député* (member of parliament) for his native Castres in 1885. Jaurès soon became a noted speaker and journalist on socialist and humanitarian issues. He attracted more public attention (most of it hostile at first) during the notorious *Affaire Dreyfus* (1894 to 1899) for his vociferous support of Dreyfus, a Jewish army officer who was imprisoned on charges of spying (later proved to be unfounded) and vilified during a nationwide wave of anti-Semitism. In 1904 Jaurès founded the Communist daily newspaper *l'Humanité*, still going strong, and in 1905 was elected head of the Socialist International. He wrote an influential *History of Socialism*, and campaigned vigorously against Europe's (including France's) rising tide of nationalism and militarism which he predicted would culminate in war. An assassin finally silenced him in a café in Paris on 31st July 1914, as the first world war broke out.

perhaps, his work) is known to everyone in France. His backstreet birthplace does have a plaque, but the house is much changed. The town's large main square is fittingly named place Jean Jaurès; several times a week it is filled with the brightly coloured awnings of market stalls which press up against the splashing waters of a fountain.

Within a few minutes of Castres, the quiet D622 crosses the border of the Regional Park and has entered the **Sidobre** hills, a peaceful area of beech, oak, chestnut and Mediterranean pine woods and flowery meadows, but noted above all for its curious *rocs tremblants*, rocking stones. One of these lies (or rather, is poised precariously!) close to D622, just to the left of the road down a track. Called 'Sept-Faux', it consists of two massive boulders, one on the other, the lower one balanced insecurely on the ground. Although no doubt this arrangement has been in place for millennia, it looks so liable to topple over that some visitors refuse to approach! Equally spectacular sights are not far away. Take D30, the next left turn off D622, and stop where the sign announces 'Rivière de Rochers'. There are many *rivières de rochers*, 'rivers of rocks', in the area — this one is called the Chaos de la Resle (or Resse or Feuillebois). It is a fantastic phenomenon, a 'river' of enormous boulders tossed down like pebbles along the narrow valley of a stream. Farther along the road, a track to the right approaches 'Le Roc Clabat', also known as Peyro Clabado. Scramble up on foot the last few metres to see these rocks doing the most extraordinary balancing act, with a giant resting on a smaller group. On top, thrown on, to

gain luck in love I have heard, are scores of small stones. If your stone stays on, the omens are good. If it falls off, the signs are less hopeful. Farther on (turn right onto the twisting D58 towards Brassac), the precarious slabs of the 'Trois-Fromages', three cheeses, piled one on the other, and the 'Roc de l'Oie', goose rock, stand just to the right of the road, their names giving over-imaginative clues to the shape of the stones.

Inevitably, quarrying for granite has scarred the Sidobre in places, and there is some logging, as can be seen at times on the way to **Brassac**. This village within the Regional Park is not unattractive at its centre, where two bridges, one of them Gothic, cross the Agout. A small château, now housing the village post office among other things, fronts onto the river. There are several little hotels and, all around, green hills. In every direction from Brassac minor roads head into picturesque country: D62 down to the Lac de la Raviège; D53 across less rocky wooded hills towards the town of Mazamet; D68 via the pretty Somail hills to pleasant St. Pons-de-Thomières; D622 over the higher and more barren Monts de Lacaune and Monts de l'Espinouse to Bédarieux. This last route passes through **Lacaune**, a small former spa on the river Gijou, which makes an ideal starting point for cool hill walks. To judge from an unusual inscription on a fountain of 1399, the town's mineral-rich waters are considered to have diuretic properties.

As the Lacaune road (D622) continues over the hills, a left turn (D53)

Overleaf: On Larzac — largest of the Causses

45

Haut Languedoc Regional Park

The Parc Naturel Régional du Haut Languedoc, the 'Regional Nature Park', was created in 1972 to preserve the flora and fauna of the little-developed forests and hills of the wildest countryside of the southern part of the Languedoc uplands — the Montagne Noire, the Monts de l'Espinouse, the Caroux and Somail massifs, the Sidobre, and parts of the Monts de Lacaune. In total, the Park encompasses some 133,650 hectares. A well as being of academic interest, with a wildlife research centre within its borders, the Park offers numerous leisure possibilities, for example footpaths, riding and watersports. Among the creatures you might see here are mouflons, those forerunners of today's sheep, as well as *sangliers* (wild boar) and eagles.

The headquarters of the Park administration, and the address for all enquiries is Parc Régional, 13 rue du Cloître, St. Pons 34220 (67. 97. 02. 10).

presses farther north into ever more remote and rustic countryside which feels worlds away from the Mediterranean. An objective to aim for, if you come exploring in this part of Haut Languedoc, is the Abbaye de Sylvanès. This Cistercian abbey is one of the least grand, most exquisitely simple of monastic buildings. Inside the abbey church there's a curious small Black Virgin in Auvergne style. The bare stone church, with its single broad nave, together with a remnant of beautiful cloister looking out over a meadow with birds singing, and a vaulted Scriptorium, all survive from the 12th century. A later addition is the lovely 17th-century Logis Abbatiale. In 1975 this was all deserted and becoming ruins; restoration work lasted twelve years. Now cared for as it deserves, Sylvanès hosts summer performances of classical music, Gregorian chants, painting exhibitions and other events.

Beyond, narrow little-used country lanes reach the heavily wooded valley of the Sorgues, winding along the edge of Larzac. There are several picturesque small villages. Take side turnings and you enter an intriguingly traditional world. That it still exists at all seems astonishing; a shepherd lounging in a lonely sunlit meadow surrounded by sheep and holding a crook; a door with the feet of a wild boar nailed to it; young women washing clothes at a public *lavoir*. One could keep going in this direction and, eventually reaching D999, turn right for Roquefort, Larzac and Millau (p. 54).

An enjoyable if less rustic journey can be made simply by staying on the main Castres-St. Pons road, N112, which follows a flatter course along the Thoré valley, the hills rising to either side. Admittedly **Mazamet**, the first town on the way, is industrial and not terribly interesting. It is, however, enclosed by the superb **Montagne Noire** countryside, and if I had to be a factory worker and had any choice in the matter I might, after all, opt to be employed in Mazamet. Overlooking it, ruined Hautpoul was the original site of the town, destroyed by Simon de Montfort. To the south, spectacular winding roads find their way across the gorgeous Montagne Noire landscape, sometimes rising high to give magnificent views, or descending along valleys hemmed in by cliffs, or passing through lovely rustic villages. If heading this way down to Carcassonne, take D118 as far as Les Martyrs, where turn left onto the smaller D101. This makes a wonderful drive. Pause at **Mas-Cabardès** to see the unusual Gothic church. Soon after, a steep footpath climbs for a kilometre up the hillside to the craggy ruined towers of Lastours château, besieged but never taken by Simon de Montfort, although the local lord surrendered the castle in 1211.

Sheep at a lavogne *(dewpond) on the plateau at Larzac*

East from Mazamet, N112 cuts a corridor through the Regional Park, which lies on both sides of the highway. Not until the Col de Fenille — which is the watershed between the Atlantic and the Mediterranean — does the road abandon the Thoré and penetrate into the Park itself, descending from the Col into **St. Pons-de-Thomières**. Administrative capital of the Park, St. Pons is an agreeable local agricultural centre in a delightful location. It is certainly not unknown to tourists, and has several hotels. The town does make an ideal base for walking, or touring by car, especially in the chestnut-covered Mont Somail country immediately to the north; there is even a Chestnut Festival in October. Traditional dances, too, are celebrated at the Folk Festival, held on the second to the last Sunday in July. At St. Pons, N112 turns away south towards the plain, while D908 begins

its journey beside the river Jaur through beautiful hills. Left of the road the Monts de l'Espinouse rise up alternately forested and bare, while in gardens and farms between the villages there are masses of almond trees; in spring they make a sea of white blossom.

Do not be tempted to drive straight past **Olargues** without pausing for a closer look. Even by the standards of this scenic region, it comes as a surprise. A picturesque old village with cobbled alleyways and steps which sometimes tunnel under houses, Olargues spills down a hillside to a sharp bend in the sparkling, splashing Jaur. An unusual and graceful pedestrian bridge, built in the 12th century, crosses the river. At the top of the village a ruined 11th-century tower still keeps watch over the countryside.

The Jaur flows into the grander river Orb in the midst of an area of natural phenomena worth spending time over. This is all just before and around the village of **Colombières-sur-Orb**. Dominating the country is the Caroux plateau, a breakaway from the Espinouse range. Cutting into le Caroux, the Colombières gorge runs north from the village. Steeper, deeper and wilder, the Gorges d'Héric is

parallel to it. Both are accessible on footpaths from the D908. Footpaths also link the two gorges, and a good circular walk can be made taking in both rivers and crossing the Caroux: the plateau gives amazing views over the rest of the Haut Languedoc, and beyond to the Pyrenees and the sea. After floods in 1930 caused by heavy rainwater running down denuded hillsides, the Forêt des Écrivains Combattants, about 80 hectares of handsome deciduous woodland, was planted on the slope of the Caroux: surely only the French would dedicate a forest to writers who have died in battle. The *forêt* is best reached from Lamalou-les-Bains. From here the narrow D180 climbs through magnificent country to the summit of the Monts de l'Espinouse (1124m).

Lamalou-les-Bains, 'Gateway to the Espinouse', is a small spa (specialising in muscular and nervous conditions). It is startling to discover that Alphonse Daudet and André Gide both came on a cure here (but then, it *is* surprising how seriously the French take these spa treatments). Lamalou, beautifully situated, makes another good base for excursions into the hills. A *Corso Fleurie*, floral parade, takes place on the last Sunday in August.

The Orb flows on towards **Bédarieux**, an agreeable country town with some industry but a pleasant character. *La Foire au Jambon*, ham and sausage market, takes place on 22nd May. Its bridge across the river dates from the 16th century. D35 rises along the river Orb and cuts across to Lodève (p. 89), while D908 continues

Cirque de Mourèze — the village enclosed by its weird rock formations

The Sheep Economy

The thousands of sheep on the Larzac plateau illustrate the way in which Languedoc's pre-industrial agricultural economy worked. In this bleakly inhospitable landscape it would seem impossible to make a living. Hardy sheep were the only viable 'crop'. Their milk was made into cheese, and in particular was taken to the caves at Roquefort to be made into a sought-after blue cheese which could be sold for good prices. The male lambs, unwanted for milk, were slaughtered soon after birth and the leather sold at Millau, a town which supported itself by making fine quality kid gloves. The sheep's wool was sold at Lodève, noted for its textile manufacturing, which employed many people. Finally, when past their useful life as milk-producers, the sheep could be sold for meat.

to Clermont-l'Hérault (p. 92), passing the Lac du Salagou and its pretty, tranquil villages, and the astonishing rock formations of the chaotic Cirque de Mourèze, in the midst of which Mourèze village preserves a nonchalant charm.

Clermont-l'Hérault and Lodève are connected by the N9, which climbs up from Lodève on one of the most dramatic journeys in Languedoc: the Pas de l'Escalette road, which after a long climb above the valley of the Lergue, begins to twist and turn strenuously, rising steeply up the sheer side of the Larzac plateau, eventually levelling out as it reaches the top. In days now very long past, this ancient highway came to an abrupt halt on its last lap up to the plateau: for this last section of the ascent, travellers had to *climb on ladders* to reach Larzac! Hence the name, Pas de l'Escalette (Ladder Pass). All the way up the road there are stunning views down across the Languedoc plain, at least for the passenger!

The **Causse du Larzac** has a strange personality. High, remote, ascetic and mysterious, it seems to embody Languedoc's defiant independence of spirit. At first sight, the broad, undulating plateau seems an empty and featureless desert, stretching as far as the eye can see. On closer inspection though it is full of life, especially in spring and early summer, when it is covered with multitudes of tiny rock-clinging wild flowers, purple, white, yellow, blue, and tough thistles and herbs hugging the ground. Small creatures manage to thrive up here, nestling into secure hibernation for the frosty winter months, and they in turn bring the birds of prey who drift slowly above, searching the ground. There is some scattered human life, too, living in rather bleak-looking villages, and above all there are sheep. Sheep by the tens of thousands. Not plump woolly animals penned into neat fields, these are vast flocks of lean, leggy sheep which wander at will, usually accompanied by just one person — sometimes only a child.

First of the Larzac villages reached by this approach is **le Caylar**. Its name means 'rocky' in Provençal and one can see why: huge rocks, weirdly weather-carved, cluster around the edge of the village. A turn to the right soon after makes a short deviation via **la Couvertoirade**, a 12th- to 14th-century fortified Templar 'cité' — a medieval village still entirely enclosed by high ramparts. The residents have the cheek, if one may put it that way, to charge an entrance fee to enter their village; on the other hand one can see their point, since apart from the trickle of tourists there are few other sources of income here. A ruined château within the walls dates from the 12th century. The houses mostly date from the 17th and 18th centuries; many of them stand abandoned while others are newly restored. They are built of sombre dark stone and often roofed with stone as well, and most, in the traditional manner, have an exterior staircase leading to the dwelling area on the first floor, leaving the ground floor to animals and equipment. On many doors the striking 'chardon de soleil' or 'chardon des causses' thistle head is nailed. Its central ring of petals opens when humidity is low, closes when high, making this a useful weather indicator. In the village's tiny graveyard beside the unusual old church are Celtic-looking discoidal gravestones. Outside the walls is a good example of a *lavogne*, one of the distinctive dewponds used to water the sheep in this riverless limestone terrain. D185 returns to the main road.

Olargues

In the 12th century Larzac came into the hands of the militaristic and mystical Knights Templar. La Couvertoirade became one of their strongholds. Small fortified watchtowers at the limits of the Templar territories can be seen on the plateau. In the 14th century the Templars were replaced by the more charitable order of the Knights Hospitallers (of St. John of Jerusalem), whose name is commemorated in the next village, **l'Hospitalet-du-Larzac**. A turning here, D23, passes close to **Ste. Eulalie-de-Cernon**, the fortified former Commandery of the Templars, and crosses to Larzac's western edge (two more *lavognes* can be seen beside this road near the village of Viala) before plunging down to **Roquefort-sur-Soulzon**.

Though in a grand setting, facing the towering plateau across the Soulzon, Roquefort is a grim modern-looking village, dominated by the ugly industrial premises of Société (guided visits several times daily) and many other smaller cheese producers. Everything must be forgiven them, however, for the cheese they are busy making is one of the best in the world, a creamy piquant blue-streaked ewes' cheese of incomparable deliciousness. The 'factories' back onto the Cambalou caves in which ordinary white ewes' cheese is transformed naturally (by bacteria in the air) into genuine Roquefort, praised by Roman emperors and every gourmet since. Inside the kilometres of vaulted caves, workers tend the precious cheese rounds, of which over six million are produced

Pas de l'Escalette, where the road zig-zags up the sheer edge of Larzac

Cheeses on their racks inside the caves of Roquefort

annually. In view of the money to be made, it is not surprising that many attempts have been made to reproduce artificially the conditions inside

the caves, although none has been successful.

D23 meets D999, where a turn to the right leads to Millau, while to the left is the workaday commercial town of **St. Affrique** (mostly modern, but with 15th-century bridge and 15th-century gilded wooden Virgin in the church) and the valley of the Sorgue (p. 48).

From l'Hospitalet-du-Larzac, N9 — absurdly wide and straight as it streaks across the plateau — rushes on to charmless little **la Cavalerie**. In the late 1970s, the long-established army camp here, which had suddenly and without consultation been greatly enlarged, became the focus of nationwide interest and concerted political action by left-wingers, local peasants and pro-Occitan groups. It reached the point of sabotage and rioting, as well as rock concerts to raise funds, before Mitter-and promised that if he were elected to the Presidency he would return the camp to its former size. True to his word, after the election he shifted the army ... to less-militant Provence.

Chestnuts

Sweet chestnuts provide an abundant harvest on the low granite and schist hills of the Haut Languedoc. Nowadays the nuts, difficult to gather because of their prickly shells, are left ungathered and lying on the ground all autumn long, or are collected as part of a family outing on fine Sundays. But chestnut trees were not treated so indifferently by the peasantry of poorer times. Long known as the *arbre à pain*, the bread tree, the sweet chestnut provided the staple food of the region. The nutritious nuts were cooked and eaten as they were or included in other dishes, soups, savouries and sweets. Being rich in starch, they were also dried (in a special outhouse called a *clède*) and ground into a flour which was used for all baking, including the daily bread. They provided too a fodder for farm animals. In addition, the chestnut tree made ideal timber for barrels, implements and house construction.

Graffiti of the era — 'Non au camp' or simply 'Larzac' — can still be seen on walls from here to Lyon.

In an exhilarating series of curves with superb views, N9 descends from Larzac into **Millau** (pop: 22,300). The river Tarn, joined here by the Dourbie, wraps itself around this bustling, agreeable town with its pollarded *platanes*. Despite the *causses* and handsome forested hills rising away on all sides, Millau feels closer in temperament to the warm South than to the encroaching Massif Central. There's a lively out-of-doors atmosphere. Millau is, or used to be, famous for fine leatherwear, especially kid gloves. In the picturesque pl Foch the town museum has a section devoted to gloves. But apart from the unusual 14th-century octagonal belfry dominating the older heart of the town, there's frankly little to see here except the magnificent setting. On the other side of the river an archaeological site has uncovered the pottery works, famous at the time, of the original Roman camp Aemilianum Castrum.

A narrow road (D41) follows the Tarn downstream from the town, clinging to the bank as the river winds its way through a green, wooded, peaceful valley. Through a succession of rustic villages, and larger **St. Rome**, where the view of the river is especially attractive, the waterside route continues all the way into the Albigeois.

Upriver from Millau, the Tarn carves its way between the looming heights of the Causse de Sauveterre on one side and the Causse Méjean on the other; the valley walls close in and soar up to create the spectacular Gorges du Tarn, which run 70km almost to Florac in the Cévennes. A tiny road — often too busy with tourists — threads its way, sometimes beneath vast overhanging

Le Beffroi (the belfry), landmark of Millau's old town

rock, beside the river. Occasional turnings lead up to high *points sublimes* which give stunning views. The best of the gorge is between **le Rozier**, where the Gorges de la Jonte meet the Tarn, and **Ste. Énimie**, at both of which there are hotels and restaurants.

Also starting at Millau is another superb valley road, the Gorge de la Dourbie, flowing between the Causse du Larzac and Causse Noir. Not as astonishing as the Tarn canyon, but not as irritatingly crowded either, the Dourbie valley is more open, less claustrophobic, with wooden slopes rising to precipitous cliffs. Some of the rock formations along the way are startlingly 'architectural', looking for all the

Overleaf: *La Couvertoirade*

world like old houses and ruined castles. A remarkable example of this can be seen at the Chaos de Montpellier-le-Vieux, on the Causse Noir. From a distance this immense confusing jumble of overgrown weather-beaten rock could be mistaken for an abandoned city, hence the name. Locals apparently used to believe that in fact it had been a real city once, punished by God for its crimes, and subsequently a haven for the Devil. To explore it, you'll need a map — on sale at the site — as much as if it were a proper town. It is reached by tricky drives from either le Rosier on the Tarn or **la Roque-Ste. Marguerite** on the Dourbie; alternatively take D110 from Millau onto the *causse* and go straight to Montpellier-le-Vieux, descending to the Dourbie from there. It is also possible to reach the Chaos directly by foot on a steep path from la Roque-Ste. Marguerite, a marvellously located village, pretty with its round tower, and with a simple hotel.

Nant, on the Dourbie between two sections of gorge, is an ideal base for touring this part of the plateaux region. It's a pleasant, large village, with an attractive 16th-century church and an arcaded covered market in the central square. Beyond it, **St. Jean-du-Bruel** opens the way for a tour beside the impressive ravine of the upper Dourbie (on D114) as it cuts into the Cévennes National Park.

For an enjoyable journey across the southern fringe of the gentle, watery, sylvan Cévennes, marking the northern limits of Languedoc, take D999 from St. Jean-du-Bruel, via the little town of **le Vigan**, with its Gothic bridge across the Arre, and down the Hérault valley to **Ganges**.

Largely Protestant in the Cévenol tradition, Ganges is a straightforward small town, once famed for its silk stockings; they are still made here, and one guesses that there is perhaps still quite a demand for this little luxury. Heading away west, D25 follows the

Transhumance

On the first chill days of winter, at about Toussaint (All Saints' Day, 1st November), the shepherds of the Haut Languedoc gather their sheep and goats for a long journey down to warmer pastures (or slaughterhouses) on the plain. Although many now use trucks, the transhumance on foot is still seen on the descent from the *causses* and Cévennes. The huge flocks, wearing gay pompoms for identification, and kept in check by experienced dogs, always travel on traditional routes, called *drailles*, which have been used for centuries. Some are like very broad footpaths through the *fôret* and *garrigue*, while others over the years have turned from tracks to lanes and now are roads passing through villages and towns. The passage of transhumance is always an exciting and colourful event for the villages *en route*. On the first fine days of spring the return journey is made, back up to the high cool pastures of the hills and plateaux.

deep valley of the Vis (*un vis*, a screw, is a good name for this convoluted river), leading eventually to one of the most startling phenomena of all in this weird, mis-shapen landscape: the **Cirque de Navacelles**. The Vis winds about so much that at Navacelles two bends eventually joined up, abandoning the former course of the river altogether, and leaving a bizarre 'island' of river bank literally high and dry. The road gives a magnificent view of this from high above. Twisting hairpins descend to the curious *cirque*, in the midst of which Navacelles village tends its vegetables and lives its life as if there was nothing unusual about the location.

D986 leaves Ganges to the south, at once reaching the **Grotte des Demoiselles**, certainly one of the most impressive of Haut Languedoc's many 'grottoes'. A funicular train takes visitors inside a mountain, where there are immense unearthly halls hung with dripping stalactites and connected by a dark labyrinth of passageways. Emerging again into the sunlight from this subterranean world, stay on D986 as it rises and falls through dry hills matted with dense *garrigue*, passing St. Martin-de-Londres (p. 88), to emerge onto the Languedoc plain.

Overleaf, left: *The valley of the Dourbie river*

Overleaf, right: *Chaos de Montpellier-le-Vieux*

61

Hotels and Restaurants

CASTRES: Grand Hôtel, 11 rue de la Libération (63.59.00.30), adequately comfortable, very moderate prices.
Au Chapon Fin, 8 quai Tourcaudière (63.59.06.17), good food and local wines at reasonable prices.

MAZAMET: Chez Jourdan, 7 av A. Rouvière (63.61.56.93), straightforward moderately priced little 2-star Logis with pleasant rooms and good restaurant.

MILLAU: La Musardière, 34 av de la République (65.60.20.63), impressive old Relais et Château with excellent food, nice rooms, attractive gardens.
Restaurant Capion, 3 rue J.-F. Alméras (65.60.00.91), good food, inexpensive.
Hôtel-Restaurant International, 1 pl de la Tine (65.60.20.66), comfortable moderately priced hotel with excellent restaurant.
La Mangeoire, 8 bd de la Capelle (65.60.13.16), very good, unpretentious and enjoyable restaurant with inexpensive menus.
Buffet de France at the railway station (65.60.09.04), smart, moderately priced.
Château de Creissels, in village of Creissels 2km from Millau on D992 (65.60.16.59), 2-star hotel in impressive creaky old château of character, busy and enjoyable restaurant, acceptable prices.

ST. AFFRIQUE: Grand Hôtel Moderne, 54 av A. Pezet (65.49.20.44), 2-star Logis with excellent restaurant, inexpensive.

ST. JEAN-DU-BRUEL: Hôtel du Midi (65.62.26.04), cheap 2-star Logis, good food.

ST. MARTIN-DE-LONDRES: Hôtel-Restaurant La Crêche, rte du Frouzet (67.55.00.04), in 15th-century building, not expensive, with superb restaurant.

ST. PONS-DE-THOMIÈRES: Château de Ponderach, rte de Norbonne (67.97.02.57), lovely old Relais et Château in 162 hectares. Not cheap.

Museums

BÉDARIEUX: Maison des Arts: av Abbé Tarroux (67.95.16.62). Painting, sculpture, local arts and crafts. *Jul–Aug: 2–6pm; rest of year: by appointment.*

CASTRES: Musée Goya: inside former Évêché (Bishops' Palace) opposite St. Benoît Cathedral. Collection of mainly Spanish paintings with some Goyas. *9–12, 2–6 daily exc Mon (closes 5pm in winter; open Mon in Jul and Aug).*
Musée Jean Jaurès: inside Hôtel de Ville (also in Bishops' Palace). Everything concerning Jean Jaurès, his life and work. *9–12, 2–5.*

DEMOISELLES, GROTTE DES: Immense underground caverns 6km south of Ganges on D986 (67.73.70.02). *Oct–Mar: 9.30–5; Apr–Sep: 8.30–7.*

LARZAC: Eco-Musée du Larzac: at La Grande Jasse, 15km from Millau on N9 (65.60.43.58). Interesting information about Larzac. *Phone for opening times.*

MILLAU: Guided visit of the town. Start from tourist office. *10am daily Jul–Aug.*
The Belfry (Beffroi), rue Droite. Interior of this town landmark can be visited and stairs climbed to top. *Jul–Sep: 9–11, 4–7 daily exc Sun.*
Musée Archéologique: pl Foch. Displays of pottery found at Roman pottery works of La Graufesenque. Separate section on history of Millau glove manufactures. *Jul–Aug: 10–12, 3–7 daily exc Sun; rest of year: Wed and Sat pm only.*
Archaeological site of Aemilianum Castrum at La Graufesenque (across river). *Open daily exc Mon and Tue.*

ROQUEFORT: Caves of the 'Société Roquefort' (65.60.23.05). Largest producers of Roquefort cheese. *Guided visits several times daily, usually at 9, 11.45, 1.45, 5.15.* The caves of **other producers** in the village also open (less frequently) for tours.
Musée Principal: beside Mairie. Prehistory of the Aveyron. *Opening times variable.*

ST. PONS-DE-THOMIÈRES: Musée de Préhistoire: in the Mairie (67.97.02.34). Interesting archaeological displays. *15 Jun–15 Sep:10–12, 3–6; rest of year: 10–12, 2–5 on Wed, Sat, Sun only.*

Tourist Offices

CRT offices (regional information): 12 rue Foch, Montpellier 34000 (67.60.55.42); 12 rue Salammbô, Toulouse 31200 (61.47.11.12).
CDT offices (departmental information): AVEYRON — 33 av V. Hugo, Rodez 12000 (65.68.11.43); HÉRAULT — pl Gaudechot, Montpellier 34000 (67.54.20.66); TARN — Hôtel du Département, Albi 81014 (63.54.65.25).
OTSI offices (local information): BÉDARIEUX — rue St. Alexandre (67.95.08.79); CASTRES — pl de la République (63.59.92.44); GANGES — plan de l'Ormeau (67.73.84.79); LACAUNE — pl du Gal-de-Gaulle (63.37.04.98 — summer only); LAMALOU LES BAINS — 24 av Charcot (67.95.64.17); MAZAMET — rue des Casernes (63.61.27.07); MILLAU — pl des Arcades (65.60.02.42); ROQUEFORT-SUR-SOULZON — 'Halle polyvalente Conteynes' (65.59.93.19 — summer only); ST. AFFRIQUE — bd de Verdun (65.99.09.05 — summer only); ST. PONS-DE-THOMIÈRES — pl du Foirail (67.97.06.65 — summer only).
Where there is no tourist office, apply to the Town Hall (Mairie or Hôtel de Ville).

Sports and Leisure

For details of facilities for walking, riding, canoeing, etc. in the Parc Naturel Régional de Haut Languedoc contact Parc Régional, 13 rue du Cloître, St. Pons 34220 (67.97.02.10). Canoe hire is available at villages along the Gorges du Tarn.

Cirque de Navacelles, once part of the river Vis

5
The Plain

The Romans settled earliest that part of their *Provincia* which swept round in a broad, barely-undulating plain from the Rhône to the foothills of the Pyrenees. On this dry, brilliantly sunlit lowland they built several towns and two prosperous cities, Narbonne (Narbo) and, less important although it now retains the best remnants of that period, Nîmes (Nemausus). They were connected by the busy *Via Domitia* (following more or less the same course as today's autoroute A9-B9), which continued south towards Spain and Africa, and east to join the *Via Aurelia* to Rome.

Under Roman rule, the region thrived and acquired much of that separate identity and character which are its hallmark today. The Provençal language or *'langue d'oc'* evolved as the locals' spoken Latin, and much of Languedoc's vibrant way of life, as well as its olive-and-grape agriculture and style of architecture dates from those days. For this civilised plain could be said to be the ancient, original Languedoc; and all the turmoil of intervening centuries having come and gone, the same area re-emerges as the very heart of Languedoc in the modern age.

Overleaf: *Sommières*

68

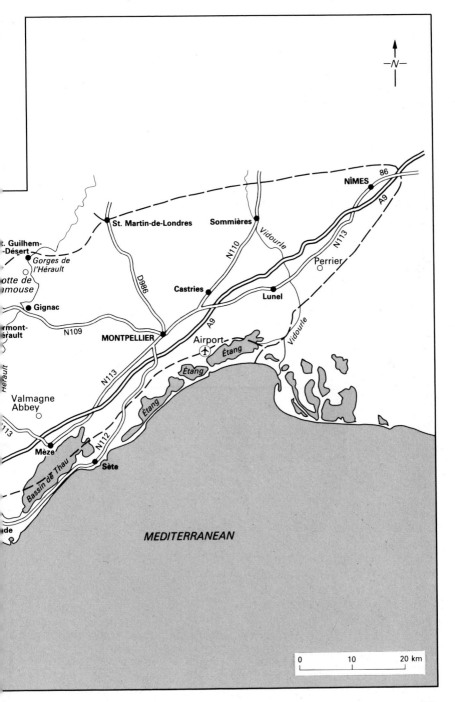

During the 4th century, the Romans' grip began to weaken. In the 5th century the Languedoc plain came under fierce attack from the northern Visigoths, and the hard-pressed Romans withdrew from the area. The Visigoths who took over from them renamed it Septimania. At first fragmenting into a multitude of contested duchies and counties and independent feudal territories, the region was gradually re-consolidated, and by the 10th century owed allegiance almost in its entirety to the expanding might of the Counts of Toulouse, known as the Counts of Languedoc.

In between the traditional stone villages and market towns and historic cities, a virtual monoculture of vineyards lies across the landscape. Kilometres of haphazard fields of vines growing in neat parallel rows create a peculiar visual impact. The distinctive patterns, geometrically precise in the detail but chaotic and unplanned in the overview, always remain as a haunting recollection of the lowlands of Languedoc. Like oases in the midst of this expanse of *vignoble*, the villages, which live body and soul from the vine, best express the spirit of the region. Though regularly enlivened by market day, or a fête, or perhaps a bit of late-night carousing in summer, these places are essentially utterly tranquil. Indeed, for most of the day, their

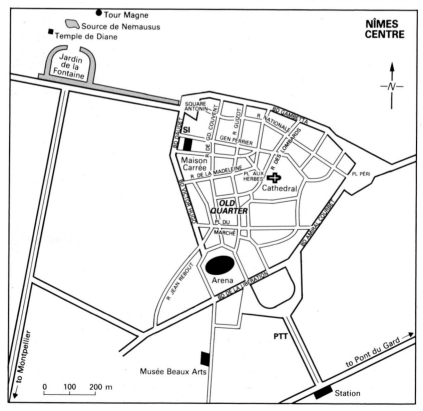

narrow medieval streets are completely silent. In the cool of the evening, the menfolk stroll to the bar to dispute and laugh with neighbours whom they have known since childhood, while the women, in leisure hours before or after the evening meal, often place straight-backed wicker chairs in the roadway outside the open front doors of their stone cottages and sit together chatting in the open air.

Tall white modern blocks rising spectacularly from the vines are the traveller's first glimpse of **Nîmes** (pop: 130,000). They make a startling contrast to the reputation of the town as a place of antiquity, and indeed, a vibrant sunny up-to-date atmosphere pervades the Nîmes of today. Much of the city's present character dates not from Roman days at all, but from booming 19th-century industrialisation. Nîmes was for many years a leading textile processing town, and after all it was here that the cloth was created which Levi Strauss needed to manufacture jeans — *de nîmes*, denim.

Bustling shopping streets and busy boulevards trace the line of now-demolished ramparts, framing the quieter medieval and Renaissance nucleus of the city. This 'Old Quarter' is threaded by narrow backstreets (many of them pedestrianised) along which stand some fine 16th- to 18th-century houses. At its heart rises a cumbersome and graceless cathedral. Originally built in 1095, but often damaged and repaired over the years in this region of religious conflict, the cathedral was almost totally rebuilt in Romanesque style in the last century. It remains grimly atmospheric inside though, very dark, with heavy Roman arches. A native of the medieval town was Jean Nicot, the doctor (!) who, in 1560, introduced tobacco into France (hence *nicotine*). Alphonse Daudet, the writer, was born at 20 bd Gambetta in 1840.

The Musée de Vieux Nîmes, in the 17th-century Bishops' Palace beside the cathedral, has a good collection of Renaissance furnishings (note the six fantastically ornate cupboards), and displays on bullfighting. In square de la Bouquerie, in 1705, towards the end of the the Camisard Wars, hundreds of local Protestants were publicly tortured and executed on the gibbet, wheel and stake. Nevertheless the city remains largely Protestant to this day. The Castellum, above the square, was the water tower of Roman Nîmes, supplied by the aqueduct which crossed one of the most magnificently beautiful pieces of civil engineering imaginable, the Pont du Gard (18km north-east of the city). In boulevard Amiral Courbet, in a 17th-century chapel, the Musée d'Archéologie et d'Histoire Naturelle provides a useful understanding of Roman Nîmes.

For the real treasures of the city are the remnants of its Roman past. In some ways this is surprising, because old *Nemausus*, although well-to-do, was a thoroughly insignificant town. It is hardly mentioned by any Roman geographer, chronicler or historian, and we know little more than that the town was noted for its large number of pensioners, its waters, its balmy climate, and hardly anything else. Yet now it has the most impressive collection of Roman buildings still standing anywhere in the world.

An inscription on a surviving Roman gate, Porte d'Arles, at the end of boulevard Amiral Courbet, records that Augustus built the walls in the year 15BC. Through this gate the Via Domitia entered Nîmes. Since that time, the arms of the city have depicted a crocodile chained to a palm tree, with the words 'Col Nem' (Colonia Nemausensium): odd, since there are not many palms in Nîmes, and still fewer crocodiles. The reason is that this was the crest of the legionaries who conquered Egypt. So grateful was Augustus that he rewarded them with villas, land, money and slaves at Nîmes, to which agreeable spot many of them then retired.

The most remarkable survivor from the period is the amphitheatre, occupying place des Arènes on the southern edge of the Old Quarter. Its exterior is sturdily graceful with high arches in two storeys, and is much better preserved than, say, the Colosseum at Rome. A lovely oval shape (133m by 101m), the interior still has rows of seats, some still marked with the line showing the space allotted to each person. Around the arena, below the seats, are fascinating vaulted corridors. Patricians sat down on the lower seats, for a good view of the contest, while plebeians were in loftier back rows. Then as now, one could pay a little more to sit in the shade of an awning.

In its heyday, this arena would have been in frequent use, and, judging by the height of the podium wall, was almost certainly primarily for contests between human beings rather than animals. Slaves and prisoners of war, for example, would have been pitted against each other, but the most spectacular and popular of entertainments here were gladiatorial combats, fights to the death between trained men (who were necessarily short-lived but achieved great fame if they should happen to survive several contests). The arena could seat about 20,000

The outer wall of the 1st-century Roman arena at Nîmes

spectators, which makes the Nîmes arena only the 20th largest in the Roman world even though it is now the most complete still in existence.

Constructed early in the 1st century, it is quite astonishingly intact despite the indignities of history. It was converted into a fortress by the Visigoths (5th century), then seized by the Saracens (8th century). They were driven out by Charles Martel, who himself then tried to destroy the structure by fire to prevent it from being taken again by the Saracens. Fortunately he didn't do as much damage as he would have liked, and during the medieval period the arena became entirely filled with houses and squalid dwellings. They were still there when Tobias Smollett visited the area in 1766, much to his disgust, but some clearance began soon after.

This ancient structure, standing in the middle of the life of the town, is once more the focus of the citizens' most popular entertainment, cruel and elegant *corridas* — traditional Spanish bullfights. They take place frequently throughout the summer (usually every Sunday).

Roman buildings are usually more awesome than beautiful, but the Maison Carrée, a temple (possibly to Youth), made of white stone, standing tranquilly by itself in a little square (off rue Perrier), is small, attractive, well-proportioned. Despite the name — square house — it's twice as long as it is broad, and appears most pleasing from the front. The extreme praise of other writers for this structure makes me wonder if my own aesthetic sense is in some way deficient. Certainly the Maison Carrée is rather nice-looking, and it is astonishing that it has survived the centuries so well. But even that most difficult-to-please author Smollett went so far as to describe it as 'ravishingly beautiful'; Henry James, too, another man who was normally not easily impressed, considered it 'perfectly felicitious'; the traveller Arthur Young wrote that it was 'beyond all comparison the most ... pleasing building I ever beheld', while Stendhal wished that an exact copy be built in Paris. Thomas Jefferson also wanted an exact copy built, but in Virginia, whither he despatched a scale drawing. And Colbert so admired the building that he declared that the whole thing should be transported stone by stone to Versailles. I confess that my own liking for this simple, elegant building, which has been standing peacefully on this spot since the year AD5, does not go that far! Gathered around outside are assorted fragments of Roman stonework, which are nothing to do with the Maison Carrée itself and do not add to its charm. The interior contains a Museum of Antiquities, with a collection of Roman sculp-

Columns of the roman 'Maison Carrée' at Nîmes

ture and a frieze of Nemausus, goddess of the nearby spring, after whom the city was named.

Nemausus' spring, now called La Fontaine, together with ruins of the adjacent Roman baths and Nymphaeum (wrongly known as the Temple of Diana), were all incorporated in the 18th century into very handsome and pleasing formal gardens called le Jardin de la Fontaine, a few minutes stroll west of the town centre. With broad steps, a circuit of waterways between stone embankments, gravelled open areas shaded by *platanes*, it is, just as Henry James put it, 'a mixture of Old Rome and 18th century France'. The spring water emerges from the slopes of Mont Cavalier, up the side of which the Jardin climbs, and at the top of which an unexciting Roman watchtower, Tour Magne (16BC), has commanding views across city and country.

Although it is 18km away from the city (take N86 to Remoulins), the Pont

Bullfights

Bullfighting, a leftover of Roman arena sports, remains a popular tradition in many towns of the Languedoc plain, which often have an arena (if not a Roman remnant, then a modern one) for the purpose. There are two distinct types of bullfighting in Languedoc. Native to the area is *Course à la Cocarde*. Lively half-wild black bulls from the Camargue are used. The men, called *Razeteurs*, dressed in white, try to remove by hand the *cocarde*, a knot of coloured ribbons, which has been fixed to the bull's head. It requires skill and daring, and injuries to the men are not uncommon. The bull is rarely hurt during the fight, although it may be slaughtered afterwards.

More spectacular is the Spanish-style *Corrida*, regularly performed in the larger arenas. On the human side are a skilled *matador* and his *peones*, *banderilleros* and horse-riding *picadores*. The bulls are specially reared young adults at the height of their vigour, chosen for their *'noblesse et bravoure'*, nobility and courage. Before the fight the bull is kept in a *chiquero*, a small dark box, to increase his disorientation when released into the sunlit arena surrounded by the cheering crowd. At first the *peones* tire the bull by encouraging him to run from one man to the other. The *picadors*, from the safety of their horses, then weaken the bull by stabbing the muscles at the back of its neck. The *banderillos* take over, planting colourfully ribboned steel-tipped spikes into these muscles. For the *faena*, the final episode, the flamboyantly dressed *matador*, concealing his sword under a brilliant cloth, takes command. His elegant movements make a dance in which the bull is his unknowing, doomed partner. At the 'moment of truth', as it is called, when the animal can go on no longer, the *matador* plants his sword skilfully between the shoulder-blades to pass directly into the heart. Less elegant, more cruel, are *Novilladas*, when young inexperienced bullfighters are pitted against young bulls.

du Gard aqueduct was essential to the very existence of Roman Nîmes. It stands at the transition from Languedoc to Provence, crossing the broad shallow Gard in its deep green valley. Immensely high and narrow, the bridge has three tiers of elegant arches, and it is especially pleasing that the arches in each tier are not all of equal width. Along the top runs a small covered water-channel, the whole purpose of the edifice. Part of a 50-km aqueduct built in 19BC merely to bring fresh stream water to Nîmes, this bridge of honey-coloured stone is as shocking as it is beautiful.

That so much labour, and such accomplishment of art and science (the structure has just the imperceptible slope required to channel the water) should be used just to carry a water-pipe across a river seems impossible. Through the aqueduct flowed 20,000 cubic metres (44 million gallons) daily. The Pont was in use for 1,000 years, of which 500 were without maintenance, and survives today in nearly intact condition. Smollett described it as 'unaffectedly elegant, simple, and majestic'. Henry James said 'It is noble and perfect ... at the same time I discovered in it a certain stupidity.' Charles Kingsley, who came here in 1863, wrote that the Pont du Gard inspired him with 'simple fear'. It is easy to imagine that his reaction must have echoed that of local tribespeople in the Roman period when they beheld this evidence of their conquerors' monstrous power.

The lofty water channel can be walked through. People crazy enough walk or run along the unprotected top of the bridge, which is 3½m wide and has a 50-m drop. The sane dine at the restaurant beside the bridge.

Leaving Nîmes for Montpellier, N113 is the fastest and most direct route. 3km off the road, near **Vergèze**, a large processing and bottling plant (several tours daily) covers the natural spring of what is perhaps now the world's most popular mineral water — Perrier. Incredibly, annual sales exceed 500 million bottles. The water emerges from an underground lake at a constant 15°C, bubbling with escaping natural gases. The gases are returned to the water, providing Perrier with its fizz. If you fancy something stronger, the road then passes through **Lunel**, a small old town producing a rich and delicious Muscat wine. Lunel was once a large, important Jewish town with its own Hebrew University and Medical School. It was founded by refugees

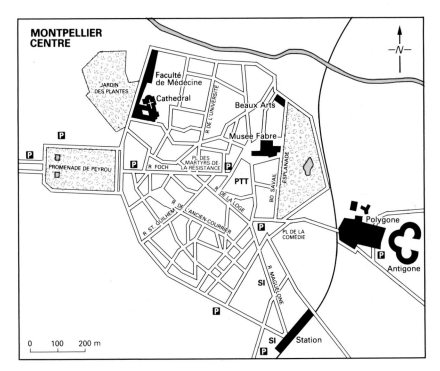

Place de la Comédie, Montpellier

from Jericho after the expulsion of Jews from Israel in the year 68. After the Jews were driven out of Lunel in 1298, it was taken over by local farmers and peasants. There are remnants of a 12th-century synagogue here.

But for preference I would take the slightly longer country road, which starts out from Nîmes as the D40. It passes via **Sommières**, an interesting and picturesque old small town, attractively sited beside a weir on the river Vidourle, at which gypsies gather to wash their clothes. The writer Lawrence Durrell has lived in Sommières, in a large detached house on the edge of town, since 1957. Here pick up the pretty N110, which meanders through vine country to **Castries**, where the château, really just a modest stately home, merits a visit. It is one of the best-furnished of châteaux open to the public, and in its attractive gardens or *'terrasses'* is a fountain supplied with water by an aqueduct which marches 6km across the neighbouring countryside. The aqueduct was specially designed for the Castries family by Paul Riquet, the man who designed the Canal du Midi (see p. 121). Soon after Castries, N110 joins N113 and enters Montpellier.

Montpellier (pop: 201,200) (p. 77) is a thoroughly satisfying city. Graceful and cultivated, yet vivacious, it is the model of how to combine past with present. At its heart (on both sides of rue de la Loge) a tangle of well-restored medieval and Renaissance streets, many of them pedestrianised, offers the stroller handsome mansions (13th to 19th centuries) to admire, often with fine courtyards open to public view, and lovely quiet back-streets and enchanting squares concealing some excellent little restaurants in which to spend a pleasant lunchtime or evening. Everywhere are surprisingly chic and pricey boutiques, revealing that there is plenty of money in the town. The old quarters — known good-humouredly as *lou clapas*, the rubble — are extensive, taking up much of the present centre of Montpellier. At their edges are some

impressive 18th-century constructions as well as startlingly imaginative modern developments, of which certainly the most impressive is L'Antigone. Tucked away behind a modern indoor shopping complex called La Polygone, the jocularly named Antigone is a vast and brand new housing estate designed by the architect Richard Bofil in a sort of neo-neo-Classical style. The centre of it is a public square called, with suitable panache, La Place du Nombre d'Or. It is not often that new buildings give such pleasure: L'Antigone should make some other modern architects hang their heads in shame.

Focus of the life of the city is the huge and gleaming marble-paved place de la Comédie, now traffic-free. Popularly known simply as Comédie, the square is also semi-officially nick-named l'Oeuf, the egg, on account of its shape. At one end of it stands the ornate Théâtre of 1889, from which the square originally took its name. Along

Montpellier: the Antigone

one side of the square scores of café tables enable you to gaze at the passers-by (and at a statue of the Three Graces). At the other end, place de la Comédie opens into pleasant public gardens, a shady esplanade, and the Polygone shopping area.

Montpellier does not have a Classical past — unlike most other towns on the plain, it has scant sign of any Roman or pre-Roman presence in the area. Indeed it has a rather unusual history, having belonged more to Spain and France than to Languedoc. Sometime before about the 10th century, two neighbouring trading centres, Montpellier and Montpelliéret, had been established here. Both attracted quite cosmopolitan and prosperous populations with considerable numbers of Arabs and Jews. The reputation of Montpellier has for centuries been dominated by the famous medical school established here before the year 1000 by a group of Jewish physicians. It is still the leading medical college in France.

In 1204 Montpellier, but not Montpelliéret, became part of the Kingdom of Aragón, and in 1262, when the Aragónese territories were divided into two, found itself in the short-lived Kingdom of Majorca. It was sold to the French Crown in a straightforward cash transaction in 1349, and the two towns were united. In the meantime a university, incorporating the medical school, had been founded in Montpellier in 1289. Rabelais studied here in the 1530s.

The city grew steadily in importance and size throughout the Middle Ages; it remained primarily a town dominated by men of learning and men of trade.

However great their wealth and education, under France's aristocratic rule this class of people had no institutionalised political power. Perhaps for this reason Montpellier was, and is still, keenly pro-Languedoc and profoundly hostile to the culture (and Church) of their French rulers to the north. It was quick to embrace Protestanism in the 16th century, giving great support to the Camisard fighters of the Cévennes, and putting up a strong fight against the French troops who came in the early 17th century to crush their heresy. Louis XIII came in person to oversee the eventual conquest of Montpellier in 1622. The fierce fighting caused widespread destruction in the city, which benefits to this day from the superb Renaissance rebuilding which took place subsequently.

The defeat of Montpellier's Protestants did not break its insistently pro-southern spirit, and it continued as a bastion of Occitan identity. In recent years Montpellier has become not only the préfecture of the Hérault département, and the administrative centre of the Languedoc-Roussillon region, but also the spiritual and political capital of modern Languedoc and of the quasi-separatist Occitan movement. The university plays a big part in this: today, with over 40,000 students, it contributes more than anything else to the character of this city, which although still actively commercial has never been much industrialised and has always managed to keep its intellectual, idealistic air.

'How I would love you to see, one day, this Museum of Montpellier!' wrote Vincent van Gogh enthusiastically to his brother Theo in 1888. The ivy-covered Musée des Beaux-Arts (or Musée Fabre, after the founder of the collection) which so pleased van Gogh can still be found in the tree-lined esplanade adjacent to place de la Comédie. It contains many excellent works by Courbet, Delacroix, Manet, Matisse, Joshua Reynolds, Degas, and many others.

More superb fine art can be seen in an unexpected place: on the first floor of the Faculté de Médecine (bd Henri IV; entrance in rue Ecole de Médecine), Musée Atger has an outstanding collection of drawings, mostly French and Italian. Also inside the medical school is a strange Musée d'Anatomie. In the boulevard outside, the Tour des Pins, once part of the city ramparts, has an inscription in the southern language to the memory of Jaime I of Aragón. Behind the Faculté de Médecine looms the 14th- to 19th-century Cathédrale de St. Pierre, which to be quite frank is not one of the great cathedrals of France. The open narthex, with excessively large pillars and flimsy roof, is particularly ill-conceived. More pleasing to the soul is the quiet and relaxing Jardin des Plantes, France's first botanic gardens (1593), just across the boulevard.

One of Montpellier's most impressive sights, the Promenade du Peyrou, rises splendidly above the Jardin. This broad 18th-century esplanade, with peaceful benches shaded by rows of fine old plane trees, and lofty views out to the distant Cévennes hills, provides a calm and refreshing retreat from the noise and bustle of the city. Surely one of the loveliest municipal water-towers ever built, the Château d'Eau, adorns

Overleaf: *The Étang du Thau: parc à huîtres with Sète beyond*

Protestantism in Languedoc

From the mid-16th century onwards, the wind of Protestantism swept through France, especially northern Languedoc, bringing Catholics and Protestants (called Huguenots in France) into open conflict. In 1589 Henri IV, a Protestant, came to the throne: by tradition only a Catholic could wear the crown, so Henri made a hasty conversion, with the famous excuse 'Paris is worth a Mass'. His presence brought a certain tolerance towards Huguenots, and in 1598, his Edict of Nantes gave them legal equality, permitting Protestant worship in certain protected towns. Nîmes and Montpellier, and many smaller places on the Languedoc plain, such as Gignac, Sommières, and Clermont-l'Hérault, were included. Catholic opposition had not died down, however, and in 1610 Henri was assassinated, unleashing a frenzy of violence against Protestant communities, who answered in kind. In 1685 the Edict of Nantes was officially 'revoked', making Protestantism a crime. In the Cévennes, the Camisards — peasant mystic guerrillas with an extreme Protestant faith — took up arms to defend their religious freedom. They received food, money, shelter and moral support from the citizens of Nîmes, Montpellier and other Languedoc towns. Just as with the Cathar heresy four centuries earlier, the authorities of Church and State regarded the extermination of Protestantism as a vital part of the subjugation of the South to northern rule. A period of extraordinarily cruel repression began, leading to a mass emigration which has left the region relatively depopulated to this day. Northern troops were billeted in people's homes, Protestants were rounded-up, tortured and executed, as with all possible force the Crown conquered Languedoc's Protestant strongholds, gradually resuming control of the region. In 1787, the Edict of Tolerance ended the official persecution of Huguenots, and many towns of northern Languedoc still remain largely Protestant.

one end of the Peyrou; it is fed by a handsome aqueduct, under the arches of which — known as *les Arceaux* — spreads a huge fleamarket every Saturday and a flower market on Tuesdays. A pompous equestrian statue of the 'Sun King' Louis XIV stands in the centre of the Peyrou facing his Arc de Triomphe (top of rue Foch), with its bas-relief brazenly commemorating the 1685 Revocation of the Edict of Nantes which had made Protestantism illegal. Some score of years later the rack and the stake were erected in nearby place de la Camourgue, and hundreds of Camisard prisoners were executed within sight of their native hills.

Many noted writers have paused in Montpellier for a season or longer, among them Lawrence Sterne. Rousseau, Boswell, John Locke, Stendhal, Joseph Conrad. Often they were attracted by the town's reputedly healthy air, although according to Murray's Guide of 1873, 'nothing can be more trying than ... its blazing sunshine, dust, and glare'! Irascible 18-century letter-writer Tobias Smollett was similarly dissatisfied with the 'pernicious' climate and dismissive of its famous doctors, but even he was prepared to admit that 'the inhabitants of Montpellier are sociable, gay, and good-tempered'.

N113 is the main road across the plain, running from Nîmes to Montpellier to Narbonne and onward to Carcassonne. After Montpellier it reaches across to the big *Étang* (or *Bassin*) *de Thau* which backs onto the seashore harbour of Sète. On reaching the *étang*, the highway looks out onto the Parc à Huîtres, the Oyster Park, as it is known — a large area of oyster cultivation visible in the hazy waters of the lagoon. **Mèze** has a lovely relaxed small harbour with three waterside restaurants facing the *étang*. Mèze turns out to be, on more thorough inspection, a surprisingly extensive little town with two appealing shady squares and an unusual covered market. It is quiet, with few tourists. Nearby Cistercian Abbaye de Valmagne (12th to 14th century) stands in the midst of vines: the handsome abbey is today a farm which sells its own wine, really surprisingly good rich dark reds. At Mèze the road turns inland for Pézenas.

An alternative, prettier and more rural route from Montpellier heads inland to discover some enticing old towns and villages. Take N109 out of the town (follow signs to Lodève). The road rises at once into a magnificent rolling landscape of vineyards and *garrigue*, bathed in warm and brilliant light. Ahead, the hills of Haut Languedoc lie along the shimmering horizon. New by-passes could tempt you to miss the towns; but they do reward a visit. At **Gignac**, to really admire the fine 18th-century bridge which crosses

the Hérault, you will need to clamber down to the riverside. A small medieval town, once a Protestant stronghold, Gignac conserves its traditional character, and has a large, busy, picturesque market each Saturday.

Four kilometres away on D32, **Aniane** is an attractive village, the oldest in this corner of Languedoc, built around a centre of medieval lanes mostly too narrow for vehicles, though most of the existing houses date from the 16th and 17th centuries. Aniane's story illustrates events in post-Roman Languedoc. In the year 777, a devout young man from a Visigoth family who had established themselves near present-day Montpellier came wandering in this remote and unpeopled terrain of rocks and *garrigue*. His name was Withiza, but he later called himself, or was called, Benoît. His wish was to found a religious retreat in this wilderness, but he needed a place, in this relatively dry area, with an adequate supply of water. Eventually he discovered, around the site of Aniane, an abundance of springs, and here founded the Abbaye de St. Sauveur. Hence his crest — now the crest of Aniane — showing a shepherd's crook made of living wood emerging from water. The springs are still here, but now most have been diverted into the village water supply. From 1590 until the present century, a community of White Penitents lived here; their church St. Jean Baptiste (but locally known as 'des Pénitents') can be seen in the old place du Marché, beside 'Les Halles', a 19th-century grain market. Nowadays Aniane is a local centre for

Overleaf: *Mèze, harbour front on the Étang de Thau*

boules tournaments. Its café tables in the shady esplanade make a pleasant spot to pass an idle moment.

D32 climbs away fom the plain into the southern fringes of the Cévennes hills, through rustic Puéchabon, and Viols-le-Fort, an old fortified village in wild *garrigue*, to St. Martin-de-Londres (the name coming possibly from Provençal *loundres*, otters), a delightful small town with arcaded houses and a triangular main *place*. Staying on the lowlands, follow the Hérault upstream (on D27), crossing it on the 'Pont du Diable' (Devil's Bridge) just at the point where the river pours out of its narrow rocky gorge onto the flat plain. Follow the narrow road as it edges along beside the gorge, passing the fantastic caverns of the Grotte de Clamouse (guided visits), to **St. Guilhem-le-Désert**.

This charming — though far too 'discovered' — village was once very isolated (hence 'le désert') and accessible only on difficult footpaths. It is strikingly situated along the sides of the Verdus, a tumbling stream running under homes, through gardens, and down to the gorge of the Hérault. Fertile cultivated land behind the village is completely enclosed by steep, high slopes ending in cliffs, known as the Bout du Monde — the End of the World. Opening off St. Guilhem's tiny main square a Romanesque doorway enters the superb Abbey Church which dominates the village. The present building, in pure Languedoc Romanesque style, dates from the 10th and 11th centuries; the rest of the abbey has disappeared over the centuries. And with extraordinary insensitivity its cloisters were only recently sold to the Cloisters Museum in New York, and taken there piece by piece.

Just enough remains to show that their removal should be regretted.

In the year 800, Guilhem 'Au Court Nez', Duke of Aquitaine, much lauded conqueror of Saracens, and military adviser to the Crown, realised that he was a spiritually discontented man. His wife was dead, and he longed to find some peaceful retreat from the world. In 804, after a short stay in the abbey at Aniane, Guilhem founded his own small community here. Despite a professed longing for meditation and quiet, Guilhem was much called upon by affairs of state, and in 806 had to travel to Rome. There he was given a small piece of wood said to be a 'relic of the True Cross'. Returning to France he placed this fragment in the monastery, so ensuring that it became a prosperous place of pilgrimage (annual procession 3rd May). The pretty village of St. Guilhem remains to this day a deeply religious community, many of the houses bearing crosses, and with a number of religious groups in residence. Each year for St. Guilhem's summer *Saison Musicale* there is a month of classical music concerts in the Abbey Church.

St. Guilhem marks the edge of the plain: above it starts the region of high plateaux, plunging river gorges, and the chestnut-covered slopes of the Cévennes. Several little vine roads return from St. Guilhem (for example, via the two better-than-average Coteaux du Languedoc wine villages **St. Saturnin** and **Montpeyroux**) to the N109 (changes here to N9), which continues some 20km to reach Lodève, passing through country much threatened by the excesses of uranium mining. Just before the town the soil has a startlingly red hue, an indication of bauxite, associated with uranium.

Village Fêtes

Almost every village on the Languedoc plain has its own idiosyncratic 'story' which is re-enacted during the annual fête. Many revolve around an animal, and probably these have some symbolic meaning which pre-dates the modern version of the story. Usually it is not a real animal, but a person disguised as one, who plays the central role in the ceremonies. At Gignac, for example, the Fête d'Âne (on Ascension day, in May) reminds the people that it was a donkey which once warned the villagers of an impending Saracen attack and so saved their lives; part of the festivities is the Bataille des Senibelets — the 'senibelets' being the Saracens, dressed in curious outfits and ceremonially beaten.

Bulls feature prominently, too, especially at Mèze for the Fête du Boeuf (19th-21st August) and the Fête du Port (beginning July) for which the dance of the bull and traditional music are performed. Baillargues has its Taureau à la Corde (6th January), and bulls enliven events at Lunel (*Pentecôte*, Whitsun) and Candillargues (14th July).

Less likely creatures also make an appearance. For the Sortie du Loup at Loupian (2nd Sunday in August) a wolf leads the ceremonies. Pézenas sees the Sortie du Poulain — Procession of the Chicken (on *Mardi Gras*, Shrove Tuesday), with the playing of traditional musical instruments. St. André-de-Sangonis has its Sortie du Cochon Noir — the Procession of the Black Pig (1st Sunday in December).

In some there is no animal, like Aniane's Branle de Chemise (around Carnival time), for which everybody dresses in nightshirts and nightcaps and walks in procession around the village carrying a candle in a candlestick!

Lodève is a busy, moderately industrial small town at the foot of the amazing Pas de l'Escalette road which struggles up onto the Larzac plateau. At Luteva this was one of the main inland towns of Roman Languedoc. It has an interesting little fortified cathedral (mainly 13th and 14th centuries), many medieval and Renaissance buildings, and an unusual Monument des Morts by Dardé. More of Dardé's work is on display in the Hôtel de Fleury (not a hotel). If you are in the area on a Saturday, come to see Lodève's large and colourful market, which is given a slightly exotic quality by the many Arabs living here. The town stands at the meeting of the Lergues and Soulondres rivers, and from embankments and bridges one can pause to watch large trout twisting and basking in their waters.

Return toward Clermont-l'Hérault, either by staying on the N9 or, better, turning off (7km from Lodève on the right) for the gorgeous drive past the Lac du Salagou and through the weird rock formations of the Cirque de Mourèze. Coming this way, just before

Overleaf: *Aniane*

The Romanesque abbey church of St. Guilhem-le-Désert

Clermont one discovers the unsettling village of **Villeneuvette**, which manages to be, to the modern eye, both picturesque and horrific. It was designed and built by Colbert in 1677 around a gloomy old cloth factory, in which all the village inhabitants worked. The place looks almost like a prison workcamp, and is entered through a gateway over which is inscribed the chilling legend 'Honneur Au Travail'.

Clermont-l'Hérault is an agreeable local capital, brought to life on Wednesday mornings by its popular market extending through all the streets and squares of the town centre. The 13th- and 14th-century fortified church, with a tall, plain interior, is in Northern Gothic style. On a crest above the town stand the ruins of its old seigneurial château.

N9 travels due south across the vines to rejoin the N113 at **Pézenas** (pronounce the 's'). Turn off the main road to enter the town, for the view from the passing route nationale gives no impression at all of what a remarkable place this is. Now just a small provincial market town, Pézenas was from 1456 to 1700 the seat of the Estates General of Languedoc, the ruling council of the region. As such it

enjoyed for much of the year an exceptionally aristocratic and prosperous character, and an active social and intellectual life. Many elaborate mansions were built here, and the central *vieille ville* — now a protected area — has hardly changed in appearance since the 16th century. The *États Générales* meetings were held in the Maison Consulaire (open for visits) in place Gambetta. Older than the rest are rues Litanie and Juiverie, a Jewish ghetto of the 14th century and little changed since. Molière, together with his theatre company, stayed in Pézenas several times, notably in 1655/56, putting on plays at the old Hôtel Alphonse (32 rue Conti) and lodging at Maison du Barbier Gély (pl Gambetta; now houses the Syndicat d'Initiative). A more modern broad central square, where a local produce market is held every Saturday, runs down to the banks of the river Peyne, tributary of the Hérault.

Béziers (pop: 78,600), 23km further along the N113/N9, is a large, thriving town, capital of the region's wine trade, and adorned with some impressive medieval and florid Renaissance dwellings, and in particular a fine main esplanade called Allées Paul Riquet in honour of Béziers-born civil engineer Pierre-Paul Riquet who built the Canal du Midi. The Canal, which so transformed the fortunes of Languedoc, has a handsome port near the town. The esplanade leads to a large public park endearingly called the Plateau des Poètes. Béziers was already well-established under the name Betera before the Romans took over and rebuilt it as Julia Beterrae in 120BC. Little survives though from that period. Today it has a lively, bright, energetic air, a great love of sport (especially

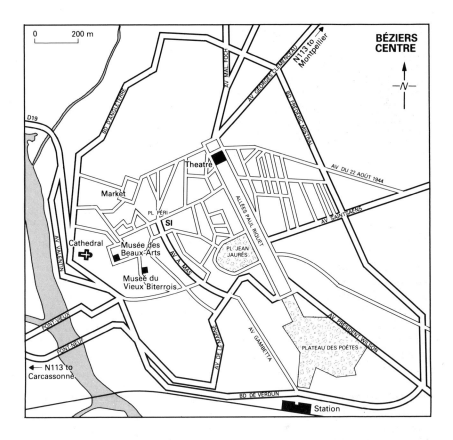

rugby and Spanish-style bullfights), and a rebellious spirit. Yet for all that there lingers over the town a certain consciousness of cruel events which took place here seven centuries ago.

For Béziers was victim of the first and most devastating attack of the Albigensian Crusaders. After their march down the Rhône valley and across the Languedoc plain, on 22nd July 1209 they arrived, eager for action, at Béziers. The Crusaders' mission was to stamp out the Cathar heresy whatever the cost, and at this point they were on the fringes of the Cathar country. It is thought that only some two hundred Cathars lived at Béziers, since this is what was shown by a list of names prepared by its bishop, but the townsfolk defied the order to hand them over and the ecclesiastical leader of the Crusade, Arnald-Amaury, Abbot of Cîteaux, gave the order which has preserved his reputation for history: 'Kill them all. The Lord will know his own.' As the slaughter began, thousands of panicking citizens pressed

Overleaf: *The pretty village and Romanesque Abbey at St. Guilhem-le-Désert*

93

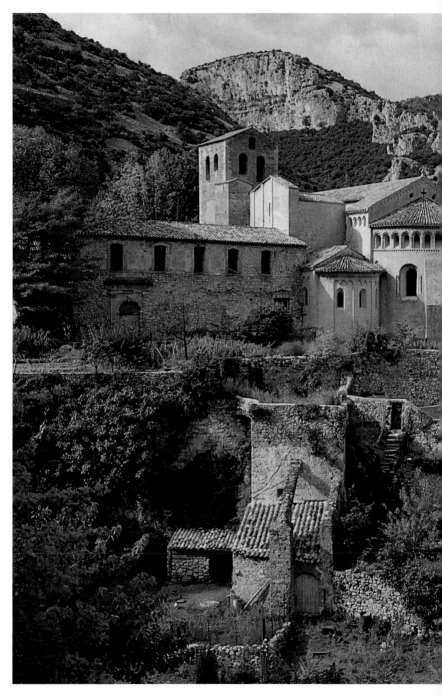

themselves into the Église de la Madeleine and the Cathédrale de St. Nazaire, believing that this would provide a safe refuge. But both were set on fire, incinerating all their occupants. It has been estimated that during the attack almost the whole population of the city was wiped out, although Arnald-Amaury reported to Pope Innocent III, 'We were only able to slay 20,000.'

The best way to understand the town's past is to visit the Musée du Vieux Biterrois, which also has a section on the Canal du Midi and another on local wine. Behind the huge and ornate cathedral, largely rebuilt in Gothic style after the Crusade, there is a good Musée des Beaux-Arts. Below the cathedral flows the river Orb, crossed by the Pont-Neuf (1846) and the 13th-century Pont Vieux, which

Statue of Paul Riquet, engineer of the Canal du Midi, in his native city of Béziers

Typical doorway in Narbonne

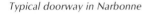

both give an excellent view of Béziers.

Just 10km out of town, on a distinctive ridge of land rising to the right of N113/N9, there stood for 700 years a thriving small town (from the 6th century BC until the 1st century AD). The site, now called the **Oppidum d'Ensérune**, has been, and is still being, excavated and opened to public view. Footways lead around those parts of the site which may be visited. These reveal with great clarity the ruins of actual dwellings from the period, the interior walls of some houses still discernible, and in particular vast earthenware storage pots can be seen, half-buried in the ground as they would have been at the time. A museum on the site displays objects discovered here, being one of the most important collections of that era, and illustrates the separate phases of Ensérune's development. Initially Iberian Celtic, it

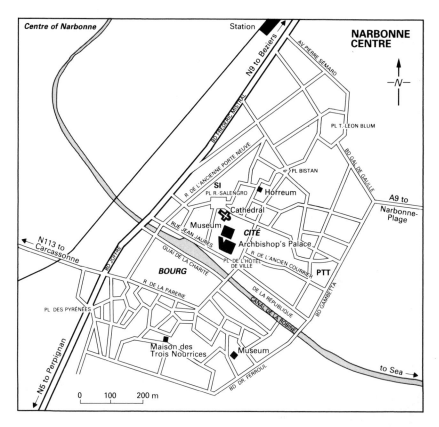

Centre of Narbonne

Station

NARBONNE CENTRE

—N—

N9 to Beziers

AV. PIERRE SEMARD

BD FRÉDÉRIC MISTRAL

PL. T. LEON BLUM

R. DE L'ANCIENNE PORTE NEUVE

BD. GAL DE GAULLE

PL BISTAN

SI

PL R. SALENGRO

Hôfreum

A9 to Narbonne-Plage

RUE JEAN JAURÈS

Cathédral

Museum

CITÉ

N113 to Carcassonne

BD. JOFFRE

QUAI DE LA CHARITÉ

Archbishop's Palace

R. DE L'ANCIEN COURRIER

PL. DE L'HOTEL DE VILLE

PTT

BOURG

R. DE LA PARERIE

DE LA RÉPUBLIQUE

BD. GAMBETTA

PL. DES PYRÉNÉES

CANAL DE LA ROBINE

N5 to Perpignan

Maison des Trois Nourrices

Museum

to Sea →

BD. DR. FERROUL

0   100   200 m

was from the first heavily influenced by the Greek presence on the Languedoc coast, and then by Gauls arriving from the north; finally, in about 118BC, the town was taken over and 'modernised' by the Romans. In addition to the considerable interest of the site itself, the Oppidum gives an amazing view of the Étang de Montady, which was drained in 1247 using channels radiating from the centre. The fields established on the reclaimed land have kept to this unusual pattern ever since. Looking farther afield, the Oppidum's panorama takes in the Cévennes to the north and Canigou to the south.

The main road carries on into **Narbonne** (pop: 43,000), once one of the richest cities in the Roman world. Gallic town Narbo, founded 600BC, taken over by the Romans in 118BC and renamed Narbo Martius, was the original capital of what was to become known as *Provincia*. Indeed Narbonne remained the principal colonial town in Gaul until overtaken by Lugdunum (Lyon) in the 2nd century AD. In AD381, the conquered lands were divided into Narbonensis Prima, with its capital at Narbonne, and Narbonensis Secunda, whose capital was Aix. The separation corresponds exactly to the later division between Languedoc and Provence.

For nearly 1,500 years Narbonne thrived as a great seaport, though the coast is now 12km away. Like many important Roman towns Narbonne had its large Jewish population of traders and intellectuals; they remained after the 5th-century Roman withdrawal, founding a university in the 11th century. While the town suffered in 1209/10 as a result of damage and slaughter inflicted by the Pope's Albigensian Crusade, even worse was the expulsion of the Jews ordered in 1306. Their departure brought Narbonne's prosperity to an abrupt end, and within 50 years the famous port had been allowed to silt up irretrievably and the university closed down. Narbonne has never recovered any importance, but is nevertheless a likeable country town, with canalside walks, attractive squares

and tree-lined esplanade. Busy boulevards with shops and cafés run where the old ramparts used to be. Le Bourg, the area south of the Canal de la Robine, is a well-restored medieval district, while La Cité, north of the canal, is the grander historic city around the enormous 13th- and 14th-century cathedral.

Large as it is, the Cathédrale de St. Just is only a fragment of what it was intended to become, for this is merely the choir of an uncompleted church whose unimaginable scale was intended to subdue any heretical leanings in the local population. Even this truncated portion of the planned edifice has, inside, overwhelming size and height, with excellent stained glass

Salasc, a pretty village near Lac du Salagou   Opposite: *Lac du Salagou*

Troubadours and Courtoisie

From the 11th to the 13th centuries Languedoc was swept by a cultural movement with spiritual, political and artistic elements: *Courtoisie* — courtliness. It elevated politeness and courtesy to a cult, and its central themes were honourable manly behaviour, chaste love, and the idea of the pure, perfect woman. Courtoisie gave rise to its own literature, all in the *langue d'oc*, mostly complex lyric poetry celebrating the brave deeds of chivalry (from *chevalerie, chevaleresque*, meaning knightly), and love stories of the greatest dignity, self-sacrifice and propriety. One of the most frequent themes was *amor de lonh*, love from afar. Not all their works were to do with love: satirical or subversive poems on political or religious themes, called *sirventes*, were popular. The long poems, called *canso*, were learned by heart and recited — or, more accurately, chanted, almost like songs — by troubadours (or trobadors) who performed in all the seigneurial courts of Languedoc, and even sometimes at village fêtes. Troubadours were always recognised for their merit rather than their social rank, and the great troubadours, who had access to the highest in their land and sometimes used their position to spread political and religious ideas, could be either princes themselves or ordinary servants. Troubadours were invited to perform in the courts of other nations, too, and their style of lyric poem, and the love themes, were the principal influence on medieval literature in Italy, northern France and Germany, ultimately having an effect throughout western Europe. Their influence can still be clearly seen in modern poetry, song lyrics and fiction.

and huge tapestries hanging. There's some good sculpture, and the elegant pale stone Chapelle de l'Annonciade has fine vaulting. In the sombre 14th-century cloisters, weatherworn gargoyles gaze at neatly clipped bushes, while next to the cathedral are shady gardens. The adjacent Archbishops' Palace contains museums of archaeology and art which reveal much about life in Roman Narbo. A bronze of Romulus and Remus, in the Palace entrance, was given by the city of Rome for the 2,100th anniversary of the founding of the Roman colony here. The former Archbishops' Kitchens now house a museum of medieval sculpture. Around the cathedral and Palace the narrow unrestored old streets of the Cité are full of interest. In rue Rouget de l'Isle, the eerie vaulted underground Horreum has a collection of Roman artefacts. The evocative little Passage de l'Ancre leads from the cathedral to place Hôtel de Ville, where the town hall, with the Source Ferriol natural spring emerging next to it, is squeezed between the 14th-century Tour de Martin and the 13th-century Donjon Gilles Aycelin (162 steps to the top).

Buildings of note south of the canal include the St. Paul basilica (12th to 14th centuries), and a superb Renaissance mansion of 1558 called La Maison des Trois Nourrices (House of the Three Nursemaids), an incongruous name if it refers to the generously

Major Festivals

Whitsun (late May)

Nîmes — Feria de Pentecôte (from Thursday before Whitsun to the Monday after): big festival with entertainments, water-jousting, competitions and bullfights.

Midsummer's Eve or Fête de la St. Jean (24th June)

Traditional bonfires and celebrations in many towns and villages. At Montpellier: bonfires, dances, music in streets all over the city.

June–July

Montpellier — Festival International de Montpellier: two weeks of dance performances and concerts.
Nîmes — Festival de Jazz: a week of jazz and blues concerts (some in Arena) with top names.

July and August

Pézenas — Mirondela dels Arts: theatrical shows, exhibitions of local arts and crafts, concerts, traditional entertainments.

First Two Weeks in August

Béziers — the Feria: lively, noisy, festival with masses of street entertainment including running of bulls.

21st–23rd September

Nîmes — Feria des Vendanges: open-air shows, bullfights, festivities.

endowed caryatids supporting the façade, since there are five of them, not three.

Between Narbonne and the sea, the Montagne de la Clape (see p. 185) is an area of hauntingly beautiful hills with a sailors' cemetery at the summit.

Beyond Narbonne, N9 and N113 resume their separate identities, N9 continuing south towards Roussillon, and N113 turning inland to Carcassonne and the heart of the Cathar country.

Hotels and Restaurants

ANIANE: Hôtel St. Benoît, adequately comfortable 1-star Logis with good restaurant, rather expensive.

BÉZIERS: Restaurant Le Jardin, 37 av Jean-Moulin (67.36.41.31), good cuisine at moderate prices.
Restaurant Le Gourmandin, 34 av Alphonse-Mas (67.28.39.18), first-class restaurant, very reasonable prices.
Hôtel Imperator, 28 allées Paul-Riquet (67.49.02.25), pleasant, comfortable, centrally located.
Hôtel des Poètes, 80 allées Paul-Riquet (67.76.38.66), modest and inexpensive hotel well-placed next to park and close to centre.

CLERMONT-L'HÉRAULT: Hôtel Terminus, in *Esplanade*, plain and simple hotel with very agreeable location and satisfyingly inexpensive restaurant.

GIGNAC: Hôtel-Restaurant Capion, on N109 opposite *Esplanade* (67.57.50.83), solid well-established village hotel, inexpensive rooms and excellent if pricier restaurant with emphasis on local dishes.

MONTPELLIER: Restaurant Le Chandelier, 3 rue Leenhart (67.92.61.62), excellent food in lavishly decorated establishment, not cheap.
Grand Hôtel du Midi, 22 bd Victor-Hugo (67.92.69.61), old hotel of character, good service, not expensive.
Hôtel Altea Polygone, in the Polygone (67.64.65.66), pricey top-class food and accommodation in city centre.
Hôtel du Palais, 3 rue du Palais (67.60.47.38), pleasant town-centre hotel, reasonably priced.
Hôtel les Arceaux, 33-35 bd des Arceaux (67.92.61.76), simple inexpensive little hotel close to Peyrou.

NARBONNE: Restaurant le Reverbère, 4 pl des Jacobins (68.32.29.18), elegant restaurant with excellènt food — not cheap.
Hôtel du Languedoc, 22 bd Gambetta (68.65.14.74), reliable adequate unexceptional hotel.
Hôtel du Midi, 4 av de Toulouse (68.41.04.62), low-priced 2-star Logis on busy road.

NÎMES: Restaurant l'Alberguier, 4 rue Racine (66.36.13.22), very good popular central restaurant with reasonably priced menus.
Hôtel Imperator, quai de la Fontaine (66.21.90.30), luxury hotel close to city centre, with first-class restaurant (L'Enclos de la Fontaine).

Pézenas

103

Hôtel-Restaurant le Louvre, 2 square de la Couronne (66.67.22.75), reliable, inexpensive hotel and good restaurant with acceptable prices.
PÉZENAS: Hôtel Restaurant Genieys, 9 av A. Briand (67.98.13.99), really likeable little inexpensive 2-star Logis.

Museums

BÉZIERS: Musée Fabregat: Hôtel Fabregat, pl de la Révolution (67.28.38.78). Fine arts, and Roman and Greek archaeological finds. *9–12, 2–6 (exc Sun am, Mon)*.
Musée Fayet: Hôtel Fayet, 9 rue du Capus (67.28.38.78). Fine Arts of 19th and 20th centuries. *10–12, 2–5 (open till 6pm in July and August)*.
Musée du Vieux Biterrois: 7 rue Massol (67.28.44.18). Very complete collections and displays concerning the history of Béziers from prehistoric to recent times. *9–12, 2–6 (closes at 5pm Oct–Apr)*.
Musée d'Histoire Naturelle: Hôtel Lagarrigue, pl Sémard (67.76.90.10). Natural history. *Mon–Fri 2–5pm only*.

CASTRIES: Le Château (67.70.11.83). *Open 1st Apr to 15th Dec: 10–12, 2.30–5,30 (exc Mon); rest of year: open for limited period on Sat & Sun only or by special request*.

ENSÉRUNE: Oppidum d'Ensérune (67.37.01.23). Large Iberian-Greek-Roman archaeological site close to Nissan-lez-Ensérune, and interesting museum on the site. *10–12, 2–5 (open till 6pm Jul–Aug); closed Sun am*.

MÈZE: Musée du Bassin de Thau: at Bouzigues, nr Mèze (67.78.31.46). Exhibitions on shellfish cultivation in the *étang*. *Phone for appointment*.

MONTPELLIER: Musée des Beaux-Arts or Musée Fabre (Fine Arts Museum): corner rue Montpellieret/bd Bonne Nouvelle (67.66.06.34). Good collection painting, drawing, sculpture, from 16th century to present day. Adjacent building houses **Musée Sabatier d'Espeyran**, private house furnished in 18th-century style. *9–12, 2–5.30 (exc Mon. Closes 5pm on weekends)*.
Musée Atger: In Faculté de Médecine, rue École de Médecine (67.66.27.77). Excellent (mainly Italian) drawings collected by X. Atger (1759–1833). *By arrangement*.
Musée de la Société Archéologique (Archaeology Museum): 5 rue des Trésories de France. Collections from prehistory, Classical period, Middle Ages. *By arrangement*.
Musée de la Pharmacie: Faculté de Pharmacie (67.63.20.47). Historical pharmacy. *Tues & Fri only: 10–12*.
Lou Fougau Mont-Pelierenc: 2 pl Pétrarque (67.60.53.73). Museum of local traditional arts, crafts and customs. *By arrangement*.
Musée de l'Infanterie (67.42.52.33). History of infantry. *Mon–Fri 8–11, 2–5 (exc fêtes)*.

104

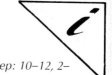

NARBONNE: *All museums in Narbonne are open 15th May–30th Sep: 10–12, 2–6; rest of year: 10–11.50, 2–5.15. They include:*

Musée d'Art et d'Histoire: inside Archbishops' Palace (68.32.31.60). 16th–20th-century painting, pottery, porcelain, sculpture.
Musée Archéologique: inside Archbishops' Palace (68.32.31.60). Local history from prehistoric to medieval times.
Musée de l'Horreum: rue Rouget de l'Isle (68.32.31.60). Underground Roman warehouse with archaeological finds.
Musée Lapidaire: Eglise N-D de Lamourguier (68.32.31.60). Gallo-Roman and medieval finds.

NÎMES: *All Roman monuments are open Oct–May 9–12, 2–5 (closed Sun am, Tues, 1 & 2 Jan, 1 & 11 Nov, 25 & 26 Dec); Jun-Sep 8.30am–7.30pm daily. Entry is cheaper if a combined ticket for all of them is bought. The Roman monuments included are:*

The Arena (Les Arènes): pl des Arènes, bottom of bd Victor-Hugo. Best preserved Roman amphitheatre in existence.
La Maison Carrée: pl de la Comédie/rue du Gal-Perrier. Best-preserved Roman temple in existence, highly praised for elegant proportions. Antiquities museum inside — note marble Apollo, bronze head of Apollo, frieze of Nemausus, white marble head of Venus.
'Temple of Diana': Inside Jardin de la Fontaine (an 18th-century formal French garden built around ruined Roman baths). Ruined nymphaeum.
Tour Magne: on hilltop above Jardin de la Fontaine. Roman watchtower with extensive views. *Tour Magne closes at noon.*
Other museums at Nîmes include:
Musée d'Archéologie et d'Histoire Naturelle (Museum of Archaeology and Natural History): bd Amiral Courbet (66.67.25.57 (archaeology), 66.67.39.14 (natural history)). Collections Roman and Greek pottery, glass, coins, etc. *Oct–May: 9–12, 2–5; Jun–Sep: 10am–7pm. (May be closed Sun am, Tues, and some fêtes.)*
Musée du Vieux Nîmes (Museum of Old Nîmes): pl aux Herbes, inside 17th-century Bishops' Palace beside Cathedral (66.36.00.64). Good collection of Renaissance furnishings and displays on bullfighting and local industry. *Oct–May: 11am–6pm; Jun–Sep: 10am–7pm. (May closes Sun am, Tues in winter and some fêtes.)*
Musée Beaux-Arts (Fine Arts Museum): rue Cité Foulc (66.67.38.21). Paintings from various European schools 15th–20th centuries. *9–12, 2–5 (closed Tues in winter, some fêtes, and sometimes for longer periods).*

PERRIER SPRING: 3km from N113 near Vergèze. Vast bottling complex over natural spring. *Guided tours at 9, 10, 1.30, 2.30, 3.30 Mon–Fri (exc fêtes).*

PÉZENAS: Musée de Vuillod St. Germain: 3 rue Albert-Paul Alliès (67.98.14.15). Collections of Fine art, 18th-century furnishings and local history. *Jul–Aug: 10–12, 2–7 (exc Tue); rest of year: 10–12, 2–6 (exc Tue & Wed).*

VALMAGNE: Abbaye de Valmagne: 8km north of Mèze, 8km east of Montagnac, 12th–14th-century Cistercian abbey church and cloisters. *15 June–15 Sep: daily pm (exc Tue); rest of year: Sun and fêtes pm only.*

Tourist Offices

CRT offices (regional information): 12 rue Foch, Montpellier 34000 (67.60.55.42).
CDT offices (département information): GARD — 3 pl des Arènes, Nîmes 30011 (66.21.02.51); HÉRAULT — pl Gaudechot, Montpellier 34000 (67.54.20.66); AUDE — 39 bd Barbés, Carcassonne 11012 (68.71.30.09).
OTSI offices (local information): ANIANE — in Les Halles (occasional, high season only); BÉZIERS — 27 rue du 4-septembre (67.49.24.19); CLERMONT-L'HÉRAULT — top of rue Réné-Gosse (67.96.23.86. Sporadic opening, high season only); GIGNAC — pl du Gal-Claparède (67.57.58.83); LODÈVE — 7 pl de la République (67.44.07.56); LUNEL — pl des Martyrs-de-la-Résistance (67.71.01.37); MÈZE — 8 rue Massaloup (67.43.93.08); MONTPELLIER — 6 rue Maguelone (67.58.26.04) and at railway station (67.92.90.03); NÎMES — 6 rue Auguste, opposite Maison Carrée (66.67.29.11); NARBONNE — pl R. Salengro, beside cathedral (68.65.15.60); PÉZENAS — Maison Barbier Gély, pl du Marché au Blé/pl Gambetta (67.98.11.82); SOMMIÈRES — 4 pl de la République (66.80.99.30).

Where there is no tourist office, apply to the Town Hall (Mairie or Hôtel de Ville).

Sports and Leisure

GOLF — Nîmes: 18-hole course near airport (66.70.18.60); TENNIS — Nîmes: 33 courts, lessons, accommodation at Les Hauts de Nîmes (66.23.14.67); WALKING and RIDING — for organised tours contact (walking) Association de Tourisme de Randonnée Languedoc-Roussillon or (riding) Association de Tourisme Équestre en Languedoc-Roussillon, both at 14 rue des Logis, Loupian, 34140 Mèze (67.43.82.50); WATERSPORTS — at Lac du Salagou, 3km from Clermont-l'Hérault.

Narbonne — courtyard of the Archbishops' Palace

6
Land of the Cathars

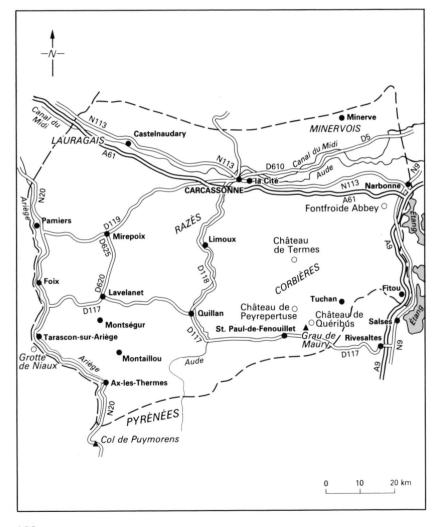

The country to the west of Carcassonne, and south from the city to the slopes of the Pyrenees, most of it now embraced by the Aude département, was the heartland of the Cathar movement. It makes a poignant tour to travel among its unspoiled hills and craggy peaks topped by gaunt Cathar castles where the rebels made their last stand. For the people of Languedoc these fortresses are the very symbol of their opposition to northern rule. Though so tranquil now, the land seems still to ring with the clashing swords of history, the march of invasion, and a people's unyielding resistance to conquest.

There is far more to this region than its Cathar past, however. The hills of the Aude département are some of the loveliest scenery in Languedoc. The wilder interior is dotted with interesting villages and hamlets. Palatable red wines are produced here, too, above the average for southern France, especially in the Minervois, Corbières and Fitou districts.

What Cathars Believed

Two gods rule creation. The evil god governs the physical world and everything in it, including mankind; everything with material form is intrinsically evil. A greater god rules the spiritual world, and has no earthly form or material trappings. Jesus Christ was a spiritual presence on the Earth. He existed only as an idea in the minds of men. He came from the spiritual world to show the way to lead a good life.

So taught the Cathars. They rejected the Old Testament, Mass, burial in consecrated ground, prayers for the dead, marriage, an organised church, and all human hierarchy as the work of the evil one.

They did not consider themselves heretics, and indeed regarded the Church of Rome as heretical. They called themselves Christians or Good Christians, and their 'priests' were called *Bons Hommes*, Good Men. Outside sympathisers knew them as Cathars (from Greek *katharos*, pure), and knew the Good Men as *parfaits*, 'perfect ones'. The creed's enemies referred to the Cathars as Albigenses.

There was only one important Cathar ritual, the *consolamentum*, initiation into a spiritual life. The Good Men or perfect ones could initiate others by baptism, laying on of hands, explanation of the arcane meaning of the Lord's Prayer, and kissing the Gospels. They formally renounced the world, thereafter keeping celibate, wearing a simple black robe, living ascetically on charity, fasting frequently, and eating no food which resulted from sexual union (meat, eggs, milk). Although Cathars opposed an organised church, the Good Men (who included many women as well) did elect local leaders whom they called Bishops. While many people were *croyants*, ordinary believers who supported the Good Men, very few went as far as becoming 'perfected' themselves until their dying day approached. Then, receiving the *consolamentum*, many would renounce all physical things until death from starvation.

The story of Catharism is a vital part of the story of Languedoc. In an age when there was no politics but religion, the real importance of Languedoc's heresy was not theological but political. The Cathar doctrine was adopted as an expression of Languedoc's separateness, a rejection of outside authorities — Crown or Church. Cathars vigorously condemned the corruption and materialism of the Catholic Church and its officials, and many refused to pay tithes, so posing a direct threat to the church establishment. It is quite certain that priests had become astonishingly wealthy and idle at this time — the Council of Avignon in 1209, in an effort to bring some Christian behaviour back into the Catholic Church, recommended that bishops should stop hearing matins in bed, stop accepting bribes, stop keeping mistresses, and try to refrain from chatting during church services! But perhaps the most important reason of all for Catharism's success in Languedoc was simply that its preachers addressed their listeners in the local language, the *langue d'oc*.

The heretical ideas first penetrated Languedoc, coming from the Balkans, in the middle of the 12th century. The whole region was quickly affected; everywhere from Nîmes to Toulouse people of all classes took up the new creed. Although outsiders called them Albigenses, after the diocese of Albi, where the first conflicts with the Catholic authorities took place, Cathars were found throughout Languedoc and were most numerous in the province's south and west.

Minerve, a wine village in the Cathar country

Not only the Church but the king of France perceived great danger in this spread of the subversive teachings. For him it might be called a foreign policy matter rather than anything to do with religion. Languedoc had a curious status vis-à-vis the French kingdom, which was much smaller then than it is today, in fact only about the same size as Languedoc itself, and with a much less thriving economy. Most of Languedoc was territory under the suzerainty of the Counts of Toulouse who, by the complexities of the feudal system, nominally paid homage or owed allegiance to the crown of France. However, they also owed allegiance to the king of England and German lords for part of their territory, and in practice a Count of Toulouse did not consider himself dependent on, or inferior to, any crowned head in Europe.

At this time it seemed likely that the Kings of Aragón, also powerful and hostile to France, were about to form a treaty alliance with Toulouse which would join Languedoc to Aragón. The Kings of Aragón already controlled a large area, including parts of France; a union with Languedoc would create a single Kingdom of Aragón from the Ebro the the Rhône — a vast, unmanageable neighbour for the French. So it was terribly important for King Philippe Auguste of France to take control of Languedoc before King Pedro II of Aragón beat him to it.

As part of his planned take-over, the King of Aragón, though doubtless a Catholic, had declared his support for the Languedoc Cathars. Pope Innocent III was a clever man, too, and in 1204, when he sent a letter to King Philippe Auguste of France proposing that they join forces to crush Catharism, he did not omit to suggest that any land which had ever been owned by a heretic, or used to offer shelter to heretics, really ought to be confiscated and added to the royal possessions.

This was a golden opportunity for Philippe Auguste to achieve his objectives. At first he delayed, being caught up with other wars, but in 1209 he and the pope launched the 'Crusade against the Albigenses' with much publicity, attracting vast numbers of volunteers and mercenaries, including many lesser nobility who hoped to be awarded various of the confiscated southern lands when the war was over.

Northern bishops and archbishops sent contingents, and the ecclesiastical leadership of the Crusade was put in the hands of Arnald-Amaury, the Abbot of Cîteaux. Simon de Montfort the Elder took overall military command. The pope granted everyone complete forgiveness in advance of all the sins which they might commit during the first forty days of the Crusade, and they set off to conquer Languedoc. It was to take over twenty years.

The first town the Crusaders reached which had any Cathars at all was Béziers (see p. 92 for full details). This large, thriving, ancient city of the Languedoc plain was only on the margins of the real Cathar territories. Many of its citizens, foreseeing trouble as the Crusaders arrived, left town for a spell. They were wise. By the end of the onslaught most of the remaining population, whatever their religion, were dead. Abbot Arnald-Amaury declared the result 'a miracle'. From the Crusaders' point of view there was some logic to this savage behaviour. After all, their mission was to bring Languedoc into the Kingdom of France without further ado. This explains the Crusaders' lack of concern about

Medieval Warfare

In the Middle Ages, wars were waged by the nobility who, under the feudal system, relied for support on those who owed them allegiance. Often this support was unenthusiastic or short-lived, and gangs of mercenaries (readily available) would be employed. They too were unreliable, leaving the battle if things looked bad or in cold weather. Weather was so important that there was a 'campaigning season' in summer, outside which warfare was almost impossible. The greatest inducement to continue the fight was the promise of lands and titles as a reward.

Retreat into fortresses was not just a safety measure. It was all part of the normal practice of medieval warfare. To seize a region and consider it conquered, an invader would have to take its fortresses. Otherwise within the territory there would remain groups capable of launching a counter-attack or cutting off lines of supply. For that reason, encounters between rival forces on a battlefield were rare: they did not solve the problem of control of the key castles.

Attackers would first surround the fortress, unless (as at Montségur) the terrain made that impossible. Tactics included undermining the walls from below, throwing heavy rocks at them from 'siege-engines' built on the spot, or using covered platforms to climb over the top of them. Defenders would fight off direct attacks, and drop rocks or fire or pour boiling oil on to 'underminers' down below. Food and water were the major pre-occupations of both sides. Often attackers could win simply by 'starving out' a castle. While they waited though, they themselves had to eat: the local population's food stores would be pillaged, but there might not be enough to feed the invading army for long.

If attackers wanted to give up, they need only ride (or walk) away. The besieged would call out for parleys to discuss terms of surrender. If they thought the terms unpalatable, they might try to escape from the castle (often easy at night). Sometimes a surrendered castle would be recaptured again later — the Albigensian Crusaders had to take some of the Cathar castles several times.

whether the people they killed were Cathars or Catholics. They were concerned only to seize Languedoc before it was too late. Certainly the decisive defeat of Béziers proved an important psychological factor as the Crusaders marched towards Carcassonne.

Probably their route was along the D5 (changes to D610), still the best road between the two towns. It passes through the superb rocky landscape of the Minervois. This district, alternating rough intractable *garrigue* with tiny terraced vineyards, produces one of the Languedoc's better wines. It lies mostly within the département of

Overleaf: *Carcassonne — the* Cité

113

Aude, but **Minerve** village itself (off the D5, reached along D607) is just over the border in the Hérault. There are some strange phenomena in this area, including the two *'Ponts Naturels'*, natural tunnels passing beneath the road beside Minerve. A stroll around the few narrow streets of the small village is enjoyable. The Romanesque church has an altar dating back to AD465, and the local museum covers the area's prehistory and also has a section on the Cathars.

Minerve was a noted Cathar stronghold. In country areas like this, Cathars and Catholics alike were invited to take refuge in the castles of the lesser nobility who wanted to protect their lands and their people, and who in any case often espoused the heretical creed themselves. The castles were often not very spacious inside, but were usually well-defended and strategically situated on hilltops. Inside these fortresses the diehard supporters of the heresy lingered on, resisting sieges and attacks, and vowing that they would rather perish than surrender. In the end — as at Minerve — many had to do just that.

The village is well-fortified even now. It stands on a high ledge of rock above a steep convoluted dry river bed, and still retains part of its formidable defences. When the Crusaders arrived in 1210 (they came back here after dealing with Carcassonne), most of the population were holed up in the castle. Even though only a fragment remains of the castle, it is easy to see that it was magnificently unassailable. Yet Simon de Montfort took the village with relatively little difficulty, simply by interfering with the castle's water supply. When the heretics emerged, 180 of them were burned alive,

although apparently they 'did not have to be pushed but, obstinate in their error, threw themselves into the flames'.

D610 meets N113, the main Languedoc highway coming from Narbonne, and the major road continues past suburbs and industrial estates into the centre of **Carcassonne** (pop: 42,500). On the way it gives marvellous, enticing glimpses of what is one of the most amazing sights in France — Carcassonne's medieval Cité. Seen from a distance it looks almost like a model, dreamlike with its turrets and castellations, too perfect to be real.

Lying about 2km south-east of the more modern Ville Basse, the Cité stands on higher ground looking over the Aude river, and is enclosed by a double bastion of awesome external ramparts. The oldest parts of the fortifications date to the Roman period. Between the walls runs a deep dry moat, and around the perimeter of both the internal and external set of defences a total of 52 sturdy towers stand guard. The city walls are entered through huge, heavily fortified gateways, Porte d'Aude and Porte Narbonne.

Established by the Gauls as Carcasso, the town was taken over and fortified by the Romans, and then occupied by Visigoths from the 5th to 8th centuries. Subsequently coming into the domaine of the Counts of Toulouse, Carcassonne was the capital of the Trencavel viscounts. The Trencavels, skilful diplomats and tacticians, so increased their domaines as to begin to have almost as much power as the Counts of Toulouse themselves. By the end of the 12th century they controlled Béziers, Albi, Carcassonne and Razés

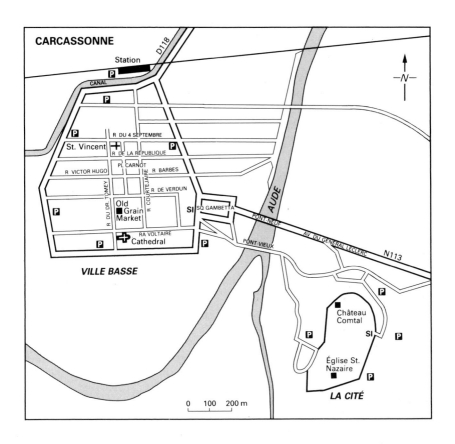

(the hill country south of Carcassonne). In effect, the Trencavels were a family growing in might and influence, and their lands harboured a great proportion of the heretics, so it was the Viscounts Trencavel as much as the Counts of Toulouse whom the King of France and the pope wanted to see beaten in the Crusade.

On 1st August 1209 the Albigensian Crusaders reached Carcassonne. Conditions inside the Cité were appalling. Far too many people had sought refuge within its walls. It was hot, and with the sanitation of the Middle Ages, the smell and flies and squalor were overpowering. Many people were falling ill, and supplies were short. Maybe the Crusade leaders felt uncertain that they could take the Cité militarily, but they proved very willing to reach a negotiated settlement with the Cité's occupants. The exact terms are not known, but one of them was that if they surrendered the citizens of Carcassonne would not be killed but would be allowed to leave 'bearing only their sins'. Surprisingly, perhaps, this agreement was fully honoured by the attackers, fresh from their bloodbath at Béziers. In the process though, they were able to capture two valuable

117

prizes: not only the Cité — but Viscount Raymond-Roger VI Trencavel himself. He died in captivity soon after, possibly murdered, and his lands and title were taken by Simon de Montfort.

In truth, the Cité is not so much well preserved as well restored. Much of what can be seen is the result of a reconstruction started in 1844 by the ubiquitous Eugène Viollet-le-Duc. Before the joining of Roussillon to France in 1659, Carcassonne had been France's most important southern defence. But since the annexation the Cité's fortifications had been neglected, parts had been demolished for building stone, and by the 19th century hundreds of poor dwellings were crammed along the length of the walls. Unfortunately, Viollet-le-Duc made certain fundamental errors in his rebuilding. For example, the shape of the turret roofs is now known to be not quite accurate, and the roofs should have been covered with Roman tiles, not slates. His mistakes are being put right, and none detracts from the pleasure of being able to see and walk around a medieval city in almost 'as new' condition.

Indeed not everyone admires the pristine neatness of the place, which after all it never had at any time in its history until Viollet-le-Duc and his successor Boeswillwald had done their work. Henry James came here in 1882, and greatly admired what he saw, yet he was troubled by 'One vivid challenge which it flings down before you: it calls upon you to make up your mind on the matter of restoration. For myself, I prefer in every case the ruined, however ruined, to the reconstructed, however splendid. The one is history, the other is fiction.'

But the Cité is no mere museum piece. Though absolutely packed, at least along the main street, rue Trencavel, with souvenir shops and camera-toting tourists, it is still lived-in to this day. There are houses and ordinary shops as well as the cafés and restaurants (predictably named after Viscount Raymond-Roger, Troubadours and even, inauspiciously I would have thought, Simon de Montfort). The church, Église St. Nazaire, beautifully combines an 11th-century Romanesque nave and 13th-century Gothic choir — after his death, Simon de Montfort was buried here; his tomb survives, but the body was later removed to his ancestral home near Versailles. The church tower has a superb view of the Cité and surrounding country. Enclosed within its own fortifications inside the Cité is the superb Château Comtal, the Counts' Castle, of 1125. The interior, with beamed halls, bare stone walls, massive fireplaces, contains a small museum (guided tours only). One place where you can get away from other visitors is in the *lices*, the broad grassy space between the walls.

On the other side of the river, the Ville Basse is the 'real' Carcassonne, préfecture of the Aude département, and itself quite historic. Its central area was built as a bastide in 1260, burnt down in 1355 by Edward, the Black Prince, and rebuilt to a slightly smaller plan immediately afterwards. Still consisting of a tight grid of narrow streets (mostly one-way driving), it is encircled by busy, noisy boulevards where the town walls used to be. The

Carcassonne — gateway into the Cité

L'Authentique Cassoulet

Cassoulet, fragrant under your golden crust,
Cassoulet, prized and blessed by everyone ...

So wrote poet A. Fourès in his Ode to the Cassoulet of Castelnaudary! While proportions vary from house to house, the basic ingredients of a traditional Castelnaudary cassoulet are always the same:
Cover dried haricot beans with cold water in an earthenware pot; boil for 5–10 minutes and drain. Cover again with fresh water.
Add plenty of bacon rind cut into large pieces. Make and add a pâté-like mixture of generous quantities of salted pork fat, a small piece of slightly rancid pork fat, and a large amount of garlic. Salt. Simmer for 2 hours until the beans are cooked but still firm.
In another (very large) pan, heat the fat out of some local Lauragais *confit d'oie* (preserve of goose cooked in its own fat), remove the pieces of meat, and in this fat lightly cook knuckle of pork, loin of pork, bacon rind and *confit d'oie*.
Make a layer of some of the cooked beans in an earthenware casserole dish; making a separate layer on top of them, put in the meats; cover in a third layer with the rest of the beans. Pepper generously.
In a frying pan, gently heat some fresh Lauragais pork sausage until juices come out; arrange the sausages in a ring on top of the cassoulet; mix them in lightly; sprinkle on the boiling sausage juices.
Place the prepared cassoulet in the oven and cook until a uniform brown crust forms on the surface; stir and allow the crust to form again; repeat several times, lightly moisten the mixture with a little hot water if needed. Continue this for 3 or 4 hours.
Serve very hot.

Ville Basse covers a surprisingly small area, and can easily be explored on foot. There are several impressive old houses, a few dating back to the 14th century. The 15th-century Église St. Vincent has, in the Southern style, a huge nave with side chapels but no aisles; high in its walls are eleven small, attractive rose windows. The 14th-century Southern Gothic cathedral has a fine octagonal belltower. The Fine Arts Museum, around the corner from the tourist office, turns out to be something of a disappointment: it displays a selection of huge canvases, some of them

quite ghastly. Most were 'given' by someone, and it's not hard to see why. More rewarding, place Carnot is the pleasant old central square, with an open-air vegetable-and-flower market, and an 18th-century fountain with a statue of Napoleon. The nearby 18th-century grain market in place d'Eggenfelden is a fine neo-Classical structure, partly still used as a market. When crossing the Aude to reach the Cité, there's no need to join the traffic hurtling over the river on the Pont-Neuf. It's just as easy to walk or drive over the picturesque Pont-Vieux (13th century), from which there is a superb view of the medieval city.

Carcassonne has, inevitably, dozens of cheap restaurants serving cassoulet, the local pork-and-bean casserole, sometimes here (but not elsewhere) including lamb as well. If you really want to find out about cassoulet at its best though, you'll have to carry on along N113 to **Castelnaudary**, birthplace and capital of this regional favourite dish. The ingredients, in proportions which are hotly debated, ideally should all be from the immediate vicinity and should be cooked in a traditional type of local earthenware dish called a *cassolo*. Subtle variations lead to vigorous disputes of almost theological intensity. While restaurants and housewives pride themselves in the deliciousness of their homemade cassoulet, nearly all the town's little charcuteries sell ready-made cassoulets for a quick family dinner. Master cassoulet chefs join a distinguished brotherhood called the Grande Confrérie du Cassoulet de Castelnaudary.

Castelnaudary is a hot, southern town, its wide main street handsomely lined with plane trees. Its citizens are traditionally known as Chauriens, and there is a picturesque old quarter. The Canal du Midi passes through the town, and many canal-travellers pause to moor in Castelnaudary's Grand Bassin, on the edge of the town centre. The képi is as much a feature of Castelnaudary as cassoulet, for a training regiment of the Foreign Legion is based here. The *Légionnaires* in always-smart cotton uniforms, crisp clean shirts and gleaming white képis add their share to Castelnaudary's character.

Castelnaudary is at the centre of the area called the Lauragais. In this district more Cathars were concentrated than anywhere else, at least in the early days. That was perhaps simply because through it ran the main road — now N113 — linking the great Languedoc cities Carcassonne and Toulouse.

Overleaf: *The medieval market square at Mirepoix*

The Canal du Midi

The Canal du Midi travels through the Languedoc countryside from Sète to the river Garonne at Toulouse, so connecting the Mediterranean with the Atlantic. Originally it was a busy water highway, and transformed the province's economy, but nowadays carries little or no industrial traffic. Built between 1666 and 1681, the Canal was the work of engineer Pierre-Paul Riquet of Béziers, who financed much of it himself. It has hardly changed since those days, and with its old arched bridges, curious elliptical locks and often tree-lined banks, it has great charm. Easily navigable for pleasure cruising, the Canal takes an elegantly meandering course. It gives a particularly enjoyable approach to Béziers, Carcassonne and Castelnaudary, with many good stopping places in the Lauragais, the Corbières, and other parts of the Cathar country. No permits are needed to use the Canal, and boat hire is available at many canal-ports along its length.

Along this highway preachers travelled, spreading the new ideas, reading Scriptures, and exhorting rebellion. Just off this road, heresy gathered momentum until small Lauragais towns like Laurac, Montréal, Fanjeaux were entirely Cathar, including not just local nobility but local priests as well. To tackle these places, when the Crusaders left Carcassonne they travelled on what is now the D119, usually succeeding in taking towns along the way without a fight.

They are agreeable, interesting places today. **Montréal**, on its lonely hill, has superb views. Apparently — so the legend goes — during a debate here between the Bishop of Toulouse (who sympathised with the Cathars) and the religious fanatic Dominic de Guzman (subsequently beatified), the Bishop's team tried to burn the paper on which Dominic had written a summary of his beliefs: the paper would not ignite, and Dominic's supporters loudly proclaimed that this showed the correctness of his arguments (this gives some clue to the standard of religious debate at that time). The event is still considered by Catholics to have been a 'miracle', as many in the town will assure you. Another hilltop town, **Fanjeaux**, was the Roman settlement Fanum Jovis, where now a 13th-century church in Languedoc Gothic style covers the site of the former temple to Jupiter. The road brought the invading army to **Mirepoix**, which also offered no resistance. If coming directly from Castelnaudary to Mirepoix, take D6 over the green hills, between the farms, meadows and woods all generously sprinkled with wild flowers.

Mirepoix is a perfect southern country town, a small *bastide*, quiet and bustling, with the Pyrenees in view. Its 15th–16th-century church, formerly a cathedral, has a single astonishingly broad nave. A pause at Mirepoix is worthwhile just to see the lovely main square, which has kept its broad covered pavements supporting heavily timbered 13th-century buildings on magnificent timber arcades. A few café tables shelter on the old covered sidewalks.

About 20km west of here, the Ariège river pours north, its valley making an historic highway through a succession of country towns. On an early visit to this edge of Languedoc, I drove to see **Pamiers**, tempted by its past importance and the role it had played in the fight against heresy. Many of the influential discussions between ecclesiastical authorities and Cathars took place here; it was at Pamiers that Simon de Montfort's claim to Languedoc lands was legally confirmed; and later the town was the base for a cruel Inquisition into heresy. Unfortunately, on arriving I found that Pamiers is a noisy, hectic town, not at all attractive. This is not simply because of modernisation, for even in 1787 the traveller Arthur Young considered it 'ugly, stinking and ill-built'. Although much damaged during the 16th-century Wars of Religion, vestiges of the medieval town do remain, and are dominated by the 14th-century octagonal brick tower of the cathedral. Turning south for the journey to Foix, there are enticing views of the Pyrenees, as there are all the way along the N20, the major road running along beside the Ariège.

First impressions of **Foix** are dramatic. Préfecture of the Ariège département, beautifully situated at the meeting of the Arget and Ariège rivers, it is overlooked by the three splendid towers of its feudal castle loftily placed on a high rock in the old town. The castle is reached up a steep walkway and is open to visitors: although most of the outer structure is older, vaulted rooms inside the towers date from the 14th and 15th centuries, like much of the rest of Foix. A museum at the foot of the central and north towers has modest displays of local culture, history and prehistory. Foix was the little 'capital' of the Counts of Foix, and it was in their county that Catharism proved most difficult finally to eliminate. Papal legates described the district as 'a nest of heretics'. Simon de Montfort passed this way, disturbed by such reports, but felt unequal to the task of an attack on the castle. In the end it escaped the Albigensian Crusaders altogether, and the County of Foix continued to deny the sovereignty of the French Crown until 1272, when Philippe le Hardi (King Philippe III) came in person with his troops and successfully forced the Count to submit. In the *vieille ville*, timbered houses line a labyrinth of lanes and narrow streets, and there are two fine covered markets which were added in the 19th century. The church of St. Volusian, often changed over the centuries, is what remains of the 10th-century Abbey of St. Volusian around which the town originated.

N20, continuing south, passes by another 'Cathar castle', the château of Montgailhard at the hill called Pain de Sucre, sugarloaf. East from here lies legendary **Montségur**, the very symbol of Cathar resistance and the independent spirit of the South. (A better way to reach the Ariège valley, in preference to passing through Pamiers, might be via Montségur.) The small, and now rather 'arty' village itself nestles down among green wooded hills. Beside it looms a precipitous rocky pinnacle, on top of which a gaunt ruined fortress stands aloof from the daily round.

After the Treaty of Meaux (1229) which officially brought the Albigensian Crusade to an end, most of Languedoc was formally placed under the authority of the French Crown. But the battle against the Cathars was in reality far from over. As the North consolidated its gains, the resistance in this corner of Languedoc became yet more dogged. French troops continued to search for Cathar strongholds and destroy them where possible. An Inquisition was set up to root out Cathars and impose suitably severe punishments. Even as the whole structure of Languedoc society was being destroyed, its lands seized, its noblemen imprisoned, pockets of unyielding opposition held on. One by one all these isolated bastions of southern nationalism and heresy were conquered.

Yet the château at Montségur could not be taken. It was the possession of Raymond of Pereille, who owed allegiance to the Trencavels. An avowed Cathar himself, he made his castle, bleak as it was, into a refuge for any Cathar, whether noble or commoner, who sought a place of safety. Eventually there were over a thousand people here. Between attacks, they would come and go as they pleased, but when besieged all would take shelter within the castle walls. Sometimes they themselves launched attacks on their enemies. The most notorious was in 1242, when a group from Montségur set off to a town called Avignonet, where Inquisitors were passing the night at a castle. Let in

by a sympathiser, the Cathars, using axes, slaughtered eleven men — Inquisitors and their staff. On the return journey, they found that news of the massacre had gone before them: villagers cheered as they passed, and a priest along the way praised the murderers and gave them a celebration meal.

However, that audacious attack led to yet another siege of Montségur. It began in summer 1243, and, as on previous occasions, the attackers tried unsuccessfully to cut off the castle's supplies of food and water. Treacherous, overgrown, easily defended paths up the mountainside, which baffled the troops, were intimately known to locals who brought the Cathars everything they needed. Through the autumn and the grim winter months both the defenders and the attackers stayed put, waiting for a change. But in March 1244 a local guide was persuaded to lead a party of soldiers up a secret path and catch the Cathars unawares. The attack was a success, leading to negotiations. It was agreed that all the castle's weary occupants would be spared if they would only renounce their faith. In the event, 205 refused to take this step, and a monument at the foot of the hill records that on this spot the unrepentant Cathars were all burned alive in the *bucher*, the pyre, of Montségur. It is still known locally as the *prat dels crematz*, field of the burned.

A difficult path leads up the vertiginous 300-metre slope to the castle (small fee charged at times: also entitles entry to museum in the village). The climb really is quite dangerous,

Foix — dominated by the towers of its hilltop fortress

and the descent is worse. At the top, the bare stone castle, now largely ruined, shocks by its small size and openness to the weather: not an enviable place to spend nine months cooped up with a thousand other people.

One lingering mystery about Montségur concerns the 'lost treasure' of the Cathars. Was this, like the Holy Grail, actually a spiritual treasure which imaginations have transmuted into something more substantial? Apparently not. Many of the Montségur fugitives were quite wealthy, and in any case contributions were constantly being sent to aid them. Yet when they descended to face their captors, the heretics had not a *sou* on them — nor was there anything in the castle. Maybe it had all been spent paying over-the-odds to locals to bring food. Perhaps indeed it was because the Cathars had no more money that a local showed the troops how to reach the castle.

Further along the Ariège valley, **Tarascon-sur-Ariège**, though now industrial, still enjoys a marvellous setting, with steep rocky hills rising all around. This is an area of *grottes*, grottoes or caves, in many of which prehistoric Man took shelter. Best of them is the Grotte de Niaux, 5km away up a mountain road which leads right into the mouth of a huge cave. Inside, wall-paintings in good condition date back 20,000 years. In **Niaux** village, the tiny Musée Paysan has displays on the popular art and traditions of the Sabarthès, as this little district is called. Connected to the Niaux cavern by underground passages, the vast Grotte de Lombrive, beside the N20 about 4 kilometres from Tarascon, has been suggested by seekers of the 'lost Cathar treasure' to be one possible hiding place.

The Pyrenees become ever larger and more distinct all the way south along this road until, at the Roman spa of **Ax-les-Thermes**, one is actually climbing right into them. As well as having 80 natural springs, two rivers join the Ariège at Ax: the town is fairly bursting with water. In pl du Breilh there's an outdoor warm pool ideal for paddling weary feet, as well as a water-pipe constantly pouring at 77°C, and a smaller pool steaming near boiling point. Ax is still immensley popular as a spa — it has three Établissements Thermals, and specialises in treating rheumatism — and as a holiday base for touring the mountains by car or on foot. In winter it becomes a ski resort. There's a casino, numerous café-bars, and though not a large town, Ax has some three dozen hotels.

While N20 carries on south towards Andorra and French Catalonia (see p. 165), the less frequented D613 from Ax rises quickly in sharp bends into the steep woods north-east of the town. After the Col de Chioula (1431m) the road levels out and crosses wide, high open pasture. Soon on the right a sign points to **Montaillou**, a tiny village of absolutely no importance (but with good mountain views). Nevertheless it is interesting to pause at this rustic community which featured in the excellent book *Montaillou*, by French historian Emmanuel le Roy Ladurie. In the 1300s there was a great revival of Catharism among peasants, priests and nobles of the County of Foix. The Inquisition at Pamiers hunted out the heretics ruthlessly, questioning everyone on what they believed, how they passed their time, where they went and

why, whom they spoke to, what was said and what was overheard. The heretics were dealt with by severe sentences, such as having the tongue cut out, life imprisonment in fetters on a diet of bread and water, or being burned alive. Ladurie's book, using these Inquisition records, which exist in their entirety at the Vatican, unveils a startlingly clear picture of life in the village of Montaillou at that time. One thing which does emerge is that not even professed Cathars really believed the natural world to be evil, while among professed Catholics there were individuals who even questioned the existence of God.

After making its way over the bleak Plateau de Sault, the road, edged with snow-posts 1½m high, reaches down to industrial **Quillan**. West from the town (on D117), the château at Puivert was a noted Cathar stronghold. South and east from Quillan, D117 passes through the narrow Défilé de Pierre-Lys, a gorge in the river Aude. Beyond, the road skirts the northern limits of Catalan-speaking Roussillon (see Chapter 7). Above, to the right, stands another Cathar castle, the ruined 13th-century Château de Puilaurens. At **St. Paul-de-Fenouillet**, the pretty little D7 makes its way through another plunging narrow défilé, the Gorge de Galamus, and comes to the Château de Peyrepertuse. Poised with gaunt defiance on a high ridge above the road, this impressive ruin was once a frontier outpost between France and Catalonia. It is now one of the largest and most complete examples of such castles (accessible from nearby Duilhac-sous-Peyrepertuse).

As the little country road by-passes Cucugnan village and threads the pass

Summer Festivals

July

MIREPOIX (during second fortnight) — La Semaine Médiévale: a colourful spectacle in which people and buildings are all in the style of the Middle Ages.

CARCASSONNE (whole month) — Festival de la Cité: artistic, musical and cultural events inspired by the city's civilisation in the time of the troubadours.

August

CARCASSONNE (first two weeks of the month) — Journées Médiévales: jousting, troubadours, archery, lightshows, entertainments of the Middle Ages and of the 20th century.

Château de Quéribus, the last Cathar stronghold, taken in 1255

A remnant of the feudal château at the village of Montaillou

called Grau de Maury, a side lane climbs steeply to the Château de Quéribus, strikingly perched on a needle-like height. Many who visit redoubtable Montségur believe that to be the last Cathar fortress to be taken. In fact, one held out longer. A few who escaped from the fall of Montségur joined a small group installed at Quéribus, and there they remained, isolated, remote, but unmolested, until besieged in 1255, when they surrendered peacefully. The fortress, now restored, is open part of the year and has stunning views.

All this dry, almost arid, rocky landscape is the Corbières, a wildly picturesque countryside of resilient *garrigue*,

*Montségur — the Cathar castle
unassailable on its high peak*

tiny vineyards, and delightful hamlets and villages. The vineyards produce some of Languedoc's best wines, robust full-flavoured reds. The best come within the Fitou *Appellation*. Turn back from Quéribus towards the villages of Cucugnan and Padern (ruined châteaux overlooking village). Ahead lies **Tuchan**, capital of the Fitou wine district (the village of Fitou itself is near the coast — see p. 185), while to the left D123 makes its way erratically across the Corbières. Where it meets D613, a left and right turn leads to the isolated Château de Termes, a magnificently fortified castle, defended by the Terminet Gorge, besieged with great difficulty early in the Albigensian Crusade. Though a mere hilltop ruin now, at that time it was an important base of the Trencavel viscounts, and the castle provided as courtly and civil-

131

Monastic tranquillity at Fontfroide Abbey, near Narbonne

ised a retreat as any for the pro-Cathar nobility. Despite problems of terrain and supplies, de Montfort took Termes in 1210; it was a heavy blow to the morale of others sheltering in fortresses previously considered impregnable.

D613 passes through picturesque, evocative **Villerouge-Termenès**, and clambers up and down the slopes back towards **Narbonne** (see p. 97). Take a short deviation before reaching the city

to see the elegant 12th-to 13th-century cloisters, church and chapterhouse of the Cistercian Abbey of Fontfroide (guided tours). The abbey is a reminder that, even in the Cathar period, the Catholic Church was not in complete disarray in this region. However, the riches and political power of Fontfroide were one of the chief causes of local grievance against the Church.

Hotels and Restaurants

AX-LES-THERMES: **Hôtel-Restaurant L'Oustal**, at Unac, village 8km north (61.64.48.44), excellent charming old hostelry in the country, well-equipped, good food, acceptable prices.

BELCAIRE: 26km from Ax-les-Thermes, 8km from Montaillou. **Hôtel du Bayle** (68.20.31.05), totally unpretentious 1-star village Logis with excellent home-cooking.

CARCASSONNE:
— *In the Cité:* **Hôtel Restaurant le Donjon**, 2 rue du Comte-Roger (68.71.08.80), straightforward, attractive old establishment with good food, reasonable prices.
— *In the Ville Basse:* **Logis de Trencavel**, 290 av du Gal-Leclerc (68.71.09.53), acceptable 3-star Logis with good restaurant, not cheap.
Hôtel Montségur et Restaurant du Languedoc, allée d'Iéna (68.25.31.41), pleasant old hotel with good, reasonably priced restaurant.
— *Out of town:* **Domaine d'Auriac**, at Auriac, 4km on St. Hilaire road (68.25.72.22), beautiful, luxurious, 19th-century Relais et Château with private gardens, excellent restaurant and peaceful location. Expensive, but worth it.

CASTELNAUDARY: **Grand Hôtel Fourcade**, 14 rue des Carmes (68.23.02.08), best hotel in town, is nothing very special but has good cassoulet and very reasonable prices.

FOIX: **Hôtel Audoye**, 6 pl G. Duthil (61.65.52.44), inexpensive 2-star Logis.

MIREPOIX: **Hôtel du Commerce**, 20 cours Dr. Chabaud (61.68.10.29), very inexpensive 2-star Logis.

PAMIERS: **Hôtel du Parc**, 12 rue Piconnières (61.67.02.58), satisfying and inexpensive 2-star Logis with good local cuisine.

QUILLAN: **Hôtel de la Chaumière**, bd Charles-de-Gaulle (68.20.17.90), inexpensive 2-star Logis with good cooking, local specialities.

Château de Peyrepertuse

Museums

CARCASSONNE: Château Comtal (68.25.01.66). 12th-century castle within Cité. Contains lapidary museum and medieval sculpture. *15th Jun–15th Sep: 9–7.30; 16th Sep–1st Jan: 9.30–12, 1.30–5; rest of year: 9–12, 1.30–5.30. Closed fêtes. Guided tours only.*
Musée des Beaux-Arts (Fine Arts Museum)*:* 1 rue de Verdun (68.47.80.90). *10–12, 2–6. Closed Sun and fêtes.*

FOIX: Le Château (61.65.56.05) and **museum of the département** (inside Tour Ronde of château): *8.30–12, 2–6.30 (closes at 6pm in winter).*
Grotte de Lombrives, near N20 south of Foix. *Guided visits. 20th Jun–15th Sep: 10–7; also visits on Sun from Easter to 1st Nov at 10.30, 2.30. 3.45, 5.* See also NIAUX, near Foix.

FONTFROIDE: Abbaye: 12th–13th-century Cistercian abbey. *Open Oct–Mar (exc Tue).*

MINERVE: village museum: (68.91.22.92). History and prehistory. *10–12, 2–7.*

MONTSÉGUR: village museum. Collection of interesting medieval itèms, mostly ordinary domestic implements, unearthed on the site of the château. *1st Jul–30th Sep: 9–12, 2–7; rest of year by arrangement.*

NIAUX: Grotte (Caves). Exceptionally well-preserved prehistoric wall-paintings. 20 max per visit, phone to reserve place (61.05.88.37). *Guided visits 1st Oct–30th Jun: 11, 3, 4.30; 1st Jul–30th Sep: 8.30, 11.30, 1.30, 5.15.*
Musée Paysan (Folk Museum) (61.05.88.36). *9–8 daily.*

PEYREPERTUSE: Le château: access from Duilhac-sous-Peyrepertuse. *Open Feb–Sep, 10–7.*

QUÉRIBUS: Le château: access by steep path from le Grau de Maury pass. *Open 1st Apr–2nd Nov: 9.30–12.30, 2.30–7.*

Tourist Offices

CRT offices (regional information): AUDE — 12 rue Foch, Montpellier 34000 (67.60.55.42); ARIÈGE — 12 rue Salammbô, Toulouse 31022 (61.47.11.12). CDT offices (information on the département): AUDE — 39 bd Barbès, Carcassonne 11012 (68.71.30.09); ARIÈGE — 14 rue Lazéma, Foix 09000 (61.65.29.00). OTSI offices (local information): AX-LES-THERMES — av Delcassé (61.64.20.64); CARCASSONNE — bd Camille-Pelletan (68.25.07.04/68.25.41.32); CASTEL-NAUDARY — pl de la République (68.23.05.73); FOIX — 45 cours Gabriel-Fauré (61.65.12.12); MIREPOIX — rue Maréchal-Clauzel (61.68.11.39); MONTRÉAL — pl de l'Hôtel-de-Ville (62.28.43.18); PAMIERS — pl du Mercadal (61.67.00.85); QUILLAN — pl de la Gare (68.20.05.63); TARASCON-SUR-ARIÈGE — av V. Pilhes (61.05.63.46).

Where there is no tourist office, apply to the Town Hall (Mairie or Hôtel de Ville).

Sports and Leisure

SKIING, WALKING AND CLIMBING in lower Pyrenees — contact tourist office at Ax-les-Thermes for details.

The Corbières hills seen from Peyrepertuse château

7
French Catalonia (Roussillon)

Languedoc, no matter how its borders are defined, has never included the area that is now the département of Pyrénées-Orientales (which is planning to change its name). This last, most southern corner of France (called Rous-sillon) was detached from Spain and joined to France in the Treaty of the Pyrénées of 1659. Though so small, Roussillon is astonishingly varied. High mountains plunge down to sun-scorched bays, ultra-modern solar

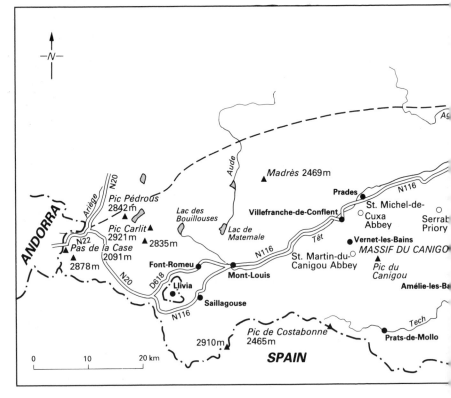

technology stands side by side with the simplest, most rustic way of life, it is exceptionally beautiful both inland and on the coast, and culturally is one of the most curious regions in the whole country.

For this is Catalonia (or Catalunya, as the locals call it). Unlike some other parts of France, including Languedoc itself, which struggle to regain or retain a sense of separate identity within the French nation, the Catalans of Roussillon feel no such need to vaunt their claims to be considered different from the rest of France. The gay colours of the Catalan flag, brilliant red and yellow stripes, fly from monuments and public buildings throughout the

region. If language is the essence of national identity, Catalans are right to feel perfectly confident that they are in no danger of being swallowed up by France. The Catalan language is very widely spoken throughout Roussillon, especially in rural districts, by people of all ages and classes. And it is not to Paris, nor even Perpignan, that the people of Roussillon look for their capital city, but to Barcelona, where today there are Catalan newspapers, TV channels, schools, and where Catalan is the official language of administration.

What is Catalonia, and where are its borders? Extending right across the Franco–Spanish frontier just as if the Pyrenean peaks presented no obstacle at all, Catalonia comprises a total of 26 provinces, of which six lie within French territory. Its northern limits are the boundaries of the Pyrénées–Orientales with the Aude and Ariège départements; while to the west it encompasses the little nation of Andorra (whose official first language is Catalan) and reaches as far as the Val d'Aren, that deep valley which cuts the Pyrenees in two and allows the Garonne river to flow from Spain into France. All the Catalan-speaking provinces, including the County of Roussillon as it was then, emerged in the 8th century from years of Arab rule as fiefdoms owing allegiance to the Count of Barcelona (until 1172) and then to the King of Aragón. Rather foolishly, King Jaime I of Aragón divided his possessions between his two sons, creating for the younger of the two, Jaime, the short-lived (1276 to 1344) Kingdom of Majorca. Jaime was given all territories north of the Pyrenees, including Roussillon, as well as the Balearics; his capital was Perpignan.

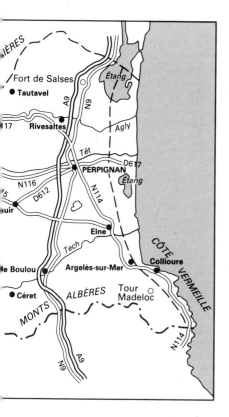

141

The Catalan Language

Most Catalans are bilingual, speaking their own tongue among themselves but knowing either French or Spanish almost equally well. Catalan is a Romance language, in other words it is derived directly from popular spoken Latin (the other Romance languages: Italian, French, Spanish, Provençal, Portuguese, Swiss Romansch and Romanian). Visitors who do not hear Catalan being spoken in shops and bars can still discover what it sounds like by tuning in to one of the Catalan radio stations. Its nearest relation is Provençal, and the resemblance to Spanish is not as close as might be expected — spoken Catalan sounds quite different, more flowing and less nasal. Many places throughout Roussillon have distinctly Catalan spelling. When reading them, note especially that:

CH is hard and sounds like 'k'
G at the end of a word is pronounced 'tch'
LL makes a 'y' sound
V is similar to 'b'
X sounds like 'sh'

A few Catalan words you might hear: *Aplec* or *Aplech* — a big festive gathering, e.g. of several circles of Sardana dancers; *Boratxe* — a bottle for pouring straight into the mouth, commonly used when people are going to share a bottle; *Cayolar* — cheese-making cabin in the mountains; *Estibe* — summer pasture; *Pla* — plateau or flat land; *Porro* or*Pourou* — another pouring bottle, this time with a spout!; *Puig* or*Pech* — mountain peak; *Riu* — river; *Trobada* — meeting, gathering.

Of course the curiously scattered new Kingdom (it also included Montpellier) was to prove quite impossible to defend. As it began to disintegrate in the 14th and 15th centuries, the whole of Catalonia on both sides of the Pyrenees formed itself into a united self-governing federation within the Aragón kingdom. That 'golden' period probably forms the basis of all subsequent Catalan longings and aspirations for a fully-fledged nationhood. However, the united Catalonia soon found itself absorbed into the Kingdom of Spain when in 1493 Ferdinand of Aragón married Isabella of Castile. The constant struggle between France and Spain for all the Catalan lands north of the Pyrenees was thus further complicated by a continual state of revolt throughout Catalonia against Spanish rule. In 1640, the Catalans rose up in armed struggle against the Spanish government, intending to retrieve their autonomous federation. Louis XIII of France cleverly took the side of the Catalans, and led them to believe that he supported their cause; indeed, by special treaty, the Catalans made the French king into the Count of Barcelona. Largely as a result of this astonishingly cynical tactic the French soon gained the upper hand, and could have taken most of Catalonia, but instead the pragmatic view was taken to follow the natural frontier of the Pyrenees. In 1659 the Treaty of the Pyrenees ceded all Spanish and former Aragón territories north of the Pyrenean summits to the French Crown.

Under the new agreement, northern Catalonia became part of France (except for Andorra and the town of Llivia). But so uninterested were the local people in these developments — for they had never regarded themselves as either Spanish or French anyway — that, it is said, only when the French Government was conscripting soldiers for the First World War did many remote Roussillon villagers discover precisely in which country they were living.

The Iberian character of Roussillon was further accentuated by the Spanish

The indomitable bulk of the Fort de Salses, guarding the ancient frontier of Roussillon

Civil War. Hundreds of thousands of Spanish communists and anarchists (both parties found themselves more acceptable if they simply described themselves as 'Republicans'), not all of them Catalan, poured over the border into France to escape the wrath of the victorious Generalissimo Franco. Between 27th January and 10th February 1939, a total of about 460,000 Spanish refugees entered Roussillon, about 10,000 of them sick or wounded. Perpignan, already the region's principal town, expanded into a large city with a vast reserve of labour — it has prospered ever since.

Anyone approaching Roussillon from the north, whether travelling on the autoroute or the route nationale, will pass the Fort (or Château) de Salses on the way. This massive defensive fortress can be seen particularly well from the autoroute (A9, 'La Catalane'). You can even stop your car at a specially designed parking area, and walk from the autoroute to visit the Fort, which is a quite remarkable construction, strangely beautiful, a magnificent piece of medieval military architecture.

The Fort de Salses, standing in the midst of vines, effectively marks the northern frontier of French Catalonia, and therefore of course was once the northern border of Spain. It was built in the last years of the 15th century, completed in about 1503, after an episode in the long running battle between France and Spain over possession of this land. In 1463, Louis XI had managed to take possession of Roussillon, but the succeeding monarch, Charles VIII, found himself embroiled in military conflicts with Italy. Wanting no distractions from his efforts there, he decided not to press

The Catalan Provinces

With the resurgence of Catalan language and culture in Spain following the death of Franco, Catalans on both sides of the border are more conscious than ever of their little 'country' as something quite separate from both France and Spain. However, while in Spain the centuries-old yearning for complete independence continues as always, on the French side of the border Catalans are not dissatisfied with their place on the remote southern edge of France, far from their rulers in Paris.

For administrative reasons the French Government considers Langue-doc and French Catalonia as a single area, Languedoc–Roussillon. But for a Catalan, Roussillon is just one of Catalonia's many provinces or districts, which number 26 in total.

The Catalan districts in France are:

Roussillon (Roussilló), the coastal plain including the city of Perpignan;
Aspres or *Haut-Roussillon,* the hills south of the Têt, extending from the plain as far as the lower slopes of the Massif du Canigou;
Conflent, the valley of the Têt;
Capcir, the upper valley of the Aude;
Cerdagne (Serdanya, Cerdan), the broad high valley of the Sègre and surrounding mountains (this area extends across the border into Spain, and also includes the Spanish enclave of Llivia);
Vallespir, the valley of the Tech.

Note though that the district of *Fenouillèdes (Fenouillet, Fenollèdes),* the hills in the north-west of the Pyrénées-Orientales département, is not Catalan; formerly part of Languedoc, it was later added to the départe-ment.

his control over Roussillon, and, on the pretext of Catholic unity and amicable relations with Spain (his nickname was 'the Affable'), simply gave it back to the now-united Spanish and Aragonese Crown. Afterwards, anxious to streng-then their defence of Roussillon, King Ferdinand of Aragón and Queen Isabella of Castile, monarchs of a united Spain, commissioned Catalan military architect Francisco Ramirez to build an unconquerable fortress on this flat, easily invaded plain.

He succeeded admirably. Enclosed within a wide moat and three sur-rounding outer rings of ramparts, the almost impenetrable central castle, surrounding a courtyard, has fortified towers at each corner. The design has due regard for cannon, which was the most modern warfare technology of his day. The whole structure is built of sturdy walls, intriguingly curved, with rounded tops and edges so that ladders would be useless, to deter attackers and minimise the damage their weaponry could cause, while aiding the occupants to fire their own cannons. Attackers who managed to penetrate the outer defences would find that they constantly had to turn corners to make further inroads into the fortress, so breaking up their assault and laying themselves open to attack. Incidental to all the military considerations, the building is a pleasure to the eye, with its intricate sysem of arches and curves, and the expanses of muted red and faded yellow brick blending in exquisitely with the golden tints of the stonework. Vauban came this way to inspect France's southern defences in 1691; he found no fault with Ramirez' design, and suggested nothing but a slight reduction in the height of the keep, probably only so that he could make his mark on the place in some way. Years later, when redundant and abandoned castles and fortresses were being dismantled all over France, these astonishingly thick (6m in places) and intricate brick walls proved too daunting for anyone to tackle them, and the Fort de Salses survived subsequent periods as a prison, a garrison, or of complete neglect, almost completely unharmed right up to the present day. Outer parts of the Fort can be visited freely, but to see the interior it is necessary to join one of the frequent guided tours.

Next to the Fort, which is on the edge of the village of Salses, there is a *cave* of the Rivesaltes vine-growers, providing a good opportunity to taste and buy some of the famous Muscat de Rivesaltes or other local wines. The 16km journey between the Fort de Salses and Perpignan crosses a flat and featureless and often windswept part of the Roussillon plain, passing **Rivesaltes** on the way. For a diversion, turn off the road and go into this windy little town, crossing a suspension bridge over the river Agly. The oldest part of town is entered through gateways in square towers. Square fortified towers are

typical of Roussillon, but these are rather interesting examples of the style. The Portail Neuf, made of red brick and curiously castellated, is especially unusual looking. Rivesaltes, like many villages in this flat coastal strip, is close to marshes and *étangs*, and at first owed its existence to the industry of extracting salt from them. The area has been inhabited (much) longer than one might suspect. A 16-km drive in the country to the north-west of Rivesaltes, in the Caune de l'Arago cave near **Tautavel**, a human skull 450,000 years old, the oldest yet known in Europe, was found in 1971. A museum of prehistory there, based on the discovery, makes an interesting excursion.

For a Catalan who knows his own land, Roussillon is not the correct name for the whole of French Catalonia. More accurately, Roussillon (or Roussilló) means only that flat, hot and now, in places, rather industrial plain around Perpignan. It is not the prettiest part of the region. The outlying villages, with their mixed Spanish and Catalan populations, preserve vestiges of charm, but closer to the city begin the extensive cheap housing estates and industrial developments. These ebb around the edges of the city. Yet, astonishingly, at its heart **Perpignan** (pop: 114,000) has many attractive corners, impressive signs of its past, and considerable character.

Although Perpignan stands on the river Têt, at the very foot of that steep valley so important to Roussillon's communications and agriculture, it is the much smaller waterway of the river Basse which more noticeably cuts through the centre of the city. Its banks have been transformed into pretty gardens (only for looking at, however,

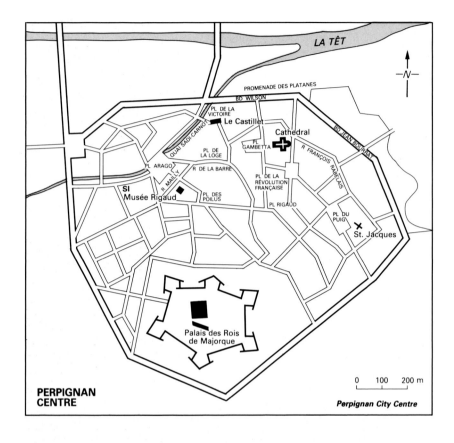

PERPIGNAN CENTRE

Perpignan City Centre

not for walking in) which run as far as a broad and pleasant esplanade of trees and fountains, an island of relative calm, called the Promenade des Platanes — its benches make a perfect spot for picnic lunch. Despite the name ('plane trees walk'), there are rows of palms and mimosa as well as lofty, handsome planes, and at its end the Promenade reaches public gardens named in honour of the Languedoc–Roussillon Resistance (Bir Hakeim).

Roussillon is a good name for this region, *rousse* meaning 'red', and the colour of earth and stone having distinct ruddy, earthenware hues.

Fittingly for the capital of such an area, many of the more ancient buildings in Perpignan's *vieille ville* are also a dusty red colour, being built either completely or partly of narrow medieval bricks, sometimes with layers of rounded stones arranged to form a simple pattern across the brickwork.

Enter the older central part of Perpignan in the proper, traditional way: through Le Castillet, the city's

Perpignan — place de la Loge with Loge de Mer on right

146

massively fortified brick gateway. First built in 1370, at about the same time as the rest of the town walls, it was originally just a bastion on the ramparts, but in 1483 was enlarged and made into a city gateway — the principal entrance into the much-besieged town. Later years saw Le Castillet serve its time as a prison, but it has now been cleaned-up, restored and turned into a pleasant Catalan Folk Museum, called the Casa Pairal (or, officially, the Musée d'Arts et Traditions Populaires du Roussillon). Le Castillet is almost all that remains now of Perpignan's medieval fortifications, which were knocked down as recently as 1906 as part of its general expansion and modernisation. Even so, the *vieille ville* remains so distinct an area, its narrow streets restricting intrusions by modern development and traffic, the sidewalks cobbled or paved with marble, and much of it reserved for pedestrians, that it feels almost as if the walls were still there.

A few paces from Le Castillet is place de la Loge, former heart of the old town. It is still a popular little square, where visitors and locals alike relax at café and restaurant tables facing some fine medieval buildings. Grandest of them is the Loge de Mer, once called, I suppose, Lonja da Mar, for during the Middle Ages it was Roussillon's Maritime Exchange. Places like this, partly administrative, partly a place for buying and selling, and partly for storage of goods, were typically Catalan; similar Maritime Exchanges have survived in Barcelona and in Majorca. Here, the ground floor used to be the Bourse, or commercial Exchange, while upstairs the Maritime Tribunal settled disputes concerning all matters relating to the sea and its commerce, which was the basis of

Roussillon's prosperity. Built of huge blocks of dressed stone, its plain exterior relieved by touches of ornamentation, the Loge was built in 1397 in Gothic style, and in 1540 substantially restructured along Renaissance lines. Today it must be one of the most magnificent hamburger joints in the world, for its arcades have been glassed-in to house a McDonald's! I could not decide whether this was an abomination, or merely amusing, but on the whole would much prefer that it had not been allowed. As a result, the interior of this fast food restaurant has a lovely marble floor and a high, beautifully beamed wooden ceiling.

Next door to the Loge stands the 16th- and 17th-century Hôtel de Ville behind massive wrought iron gates. Its façade has alternate rows of brick and round stones in the Catalan style, and within the gates is a handsome arcaded courtyard. Alongside is the Palais de la Députation, an impressive 15th-century building which once housed the permanent 'deputation' of Catalan leaders to the Aragonese Crown. Opposite the Palais, a few metres down narrow rue des Fabriques d'en Nabot (at number 2), there is another rare survivor from the Middle Ages, the Maison Julia, a 14th-century private house with a Gothic arcaded patio.

In the place de la Loge you will notice a statue of Venus, and another representing the Mediterranean in the courtyard of the Hôtel de Ville; these are by Aristide Maillol (1861–1944), the distinguished Catalan sculptor who came from Banyuls, on the Roussillon coast. He was noted especially for generously proportioned female nudes (said to be modelled on his wife) of the sort displayed here.

Twice weekly throughout the summer, the Sardana is danced in this square. It is always started off by a folk group, and soon local people will get up from their café tables, saunter over, and join in. This traditional Catalan folk dance looks simplicity itself; it is done in a circle, alternating men and women (husband always stays next to wife, with the man on the left), who link hands and perform the jigging little steps to the music of tambourine and strange flutes, notably the piercing *tible* and *flabiol*. The little group of musicians is called a *copla* or *cobla*. The tune for dancing the Sardana is light and jaunty, but repetitive and arresting and always follows a similar pattern — indeed the difference between one tune and another can be quite indistinguishable to outsiders. However, I must warn from experience that although the Sardana seems easy when one is merely watching it, the steps, in their endlessly repeated sequence, are very much quicker and more complicated than they look!

From place de la Loge, rue St. Jean leads the short distance to place Gambetta, which serves almost as a forecourt to Perpignan's Cathédrale de St. Jean. An excellent example of Southern Gothic — a style which flowed out of Catalonia (in particular, Barcelona) into the rest of the Midi — this church was started in 1324 by King Sancho, the second king of Majorca, but was not ready to be consecrated until 1509. The exterior, with two low corner towers of stone blocks (one topped by an ornate 18th-century wrought iron belfry) and characteristic Roussillon walls of thin red bricks and rounded flintstones in a herringbone pattern, is impressive enough; but walk inside to be really surprised.

Inside, typical of the aisle-less Southern style, is an immense open hall, marble-floored, dark and obscure, heavy with flamboyant ornamentation and gilt. The gloom shows off the stained glass to superb effect. The whole wall behind the altar is covered with a massive over-ornate reredos, in the centre of which a statue of John the Baptist shows him gaunt and mystical, and along the side walls are the tall, gaudy, gold-laden 16th–17th-century altarpieces of side chapels. The ceiling and walls are richly patterned, too, with vast frescoes, and hanging down are big chandeliers. To one side is an extraordinary black and white marble tomb (of Bishop Louis de Montmort). The collection of reliquaries, downstairs, is like a gilded Chamber of Horrors. A notice on the wall, signed by the present Bishop, announces in all seriousness that if visitors say an Ave Maria it will mean 50 days remission for the souls in Purgatory. A side door at the south end leads into a much older chapel, Romanesque, dating from 1025, in which is kept the agonised and lifelike early 14th-century wood carving of 'Le Dévot Christ' (the Devout Christ) on the cross. Its feet are bathed in wine on Ash Wednesday.

The chapel of Notre-Dame del Correch, beside the 16th-century organ loft inside the present cathedral, occupies part of St. Jean-le-Vieux, the original 11th-century church which used to stand partly on this site. A restored Romanesque doorway of this earlier St. Jean, with interesting carvings, can be found outside the present building.

A few minutes' walk away, place Arago has now replaced place de la Loge as Perpignan's main square. A popular spot for sitting, standing, and

149

Cloisters of the lovely former cathedral of Ste. Eulalie, at Elne

chatting in the open air, it's modern, but with some traditional character, an agreeable paved area with palms and benches, cafés and restaurants, and traffic passing by on the adjacent *quais* of the river Basse. A statue of the leading 18th-century astronomer and politician after whom the square is named — he was born at nearby Estagel — surveys the scene. The atmosphere has a decidedly Spanish flavour. Place Arago is near the tourist office, and is right on the edge of Perpignan's old central area. Close by is a museum of fine art, named in honour of the town's most successful painter, the 17th-century royal portraitist Hyacinthe Rigaud. Apart from Rigaud's own canvases, there is a wide range of other Catalan work, as well as paintings by Dufy, Ingres, Maillol, and others. A short walk farther south reaches the Citadel.

The Kings of Majorca made Perpignan their capital, so of course they had a palace here. Their small *Palais des Rois de Majorque* still stands, and is utterly charming, but is entirely surrounded and overwhelmed by the Citadel's massive brick fortifications built by Charles V (14th century) and then enlarged and remodelled by Vauban (17th century) in his characteristic star-shape. From the outside, these bare and forbidding brick walls dominate the southern part of the town centre, making it quite unappealing. It is perfectly obvious that their function was entirely military, and so they still are today, for the Citadel houses an army barracks as well as the Majorcan kings' *palais*. Indeed, over the centuries, French soldiers stationed here inflicted enormous injury to the elegant little building, which has now, thank goodness, been restored and is at last treated with the respect it deserves. The Palace consists principally of an enclosed courtyard, the focus of which is the two storey Chapel-Keep — with two chapels built one on top of the other — rising from graceful galleries above arcades. In the vaulted Hall there are exhibitions on Catalan history.

Catalans tend to be profoundly, fervently religious, and some strange local customs arise from this devotion. Few are more bizarre than Perpignan's chilling Procession des Pénitents on the night of Good Friday. The 'Pénitents' are members of La Confrérie de la Sanch (the Brotherhood of the Blood), who parade through the town, sinisterly hooded with slits for their eyes, in scarlet or black robes, displaying wax and wood carvings which they call 'misteris', and chanting solemnly. The Pénitents' religious function was to minister to people condemned to death.

The Confrérie's own chapel is an extension added to the 14th-century Église St. Jacques, on the eastern side of the town centre beside a remnant of the old city walls; there's a pleasant little park here called La Miranda. Inside the porch of the church, the weird Croix des Outrages (Cross of Insults) is displayed. This cross, on which are fixed all sorts of curious symbols and emblems, but no Christ, is carried by the hooded Pénitents on their Easter procession. Dramatic Easter processions take place in several other Roussillon towns and villages, for example Arles-sur-Tech, Collioure, Bouleternère and Ille-sur-Têt.

Just 6km east of Perpignan, on the coast road, **Castel-Roussillon** (or Château-Roussillon) was the site of the original forerunner of Perpignan during Roman and pre-Roman days. An Iberian town called Ruscino, probably dating from about 700BC, it was taken over in the 2nd century BC by the colonising Roman forces working their way around the coast. Ruscino, on the Têt, close to the mouth of the river as it was then, served as a useful trading centre and stopping place on the Romans' highway Via Domitia, which linked their bases in Spain to Provincia and Italy. Oddly and disappointingly, little survives of Ruscino, not only from the Roman age, but even the intervening centuries have left few traces. Excavations of the Roman forum, ruins of a Romanesque church, and a lonely tower which was part of the 12th-century fortifications, are all that remains of Ruscino.

Further east lie the popular coastal resorts (see p. 189) **Canet-Plage** and, to its south, the newly developed resort **St. Cyprien**. N114, the main road south to Spain from Perpignan, which is only

52km altogether, skirts the small hilltop town of **Elne**. Largely ignored by tourists, Elne is an ancient place and has considerable Spanish–Catalan atmosphere. At least 700 years before Christ it was Illiberis, a thriving seaport of the local tribes. When Hannibal came by with his elephants in 218BC, on his way from Carthage to attack Italy, the Romans tried to persuade local Iberian tribes to fight against him and check his advance. Instead, the tribes signed a treaty with Hannibal at Elne, and invited him to use the town as a base. One popular clause in the treaty, apparently, was that any dispute between local men and Hannibal's soldiery would be judged by a tribunal of the local womenfolk.

During the Roman period, when it was renamed Castrum Helenae in honour of Helen, the mother of Emperor Constantine, this little town was far more important than neighbouring Ruscino. It remained the main town in this corner of France for centuries; indeed Elne was for over a thousand years (from 577 to 1602) the episcopal capital of Roussillon. Rising above tangled alleys and higgledy Roman tile rooftops, within the ramparts of old Elne, stands its 11th-century cathedral with a sturdy fortified tower and exquisite 12th–14th-century cloisters. At first sight these cloisters, with double rows of elegant pillars and exceptionally good sculpted capitals, seem to have emerged astonishingly unharmed from the savage assault of the violent centuries which ravaged this region. In fact, though, apart from the lovely Romanesque south gallery, which is entirely original, the rest was rebuilt in Gothic style and patched up — very successfully — at various times over the years. An upper gallery was removed altogether as recently as 1827. The high terrace in front of the church has an excellent view across the town and surrounding country.

N114 continues past **Argelès-sur-Mer**, which is not on the sea any more despite the name. The heart of Argelès is an old town, with a small Musée Catalan, and dominated by the square fortified tower of its 14th-century church; but nowadays this historic centre is rather lost among its encircling new villas and holiday homes. Adjacent beach resort **Argelès-Plage** likes to call itself the 'camping capital of Europe', which to my mind is no recommendation. The main road angles down towards the coast, turning eastward to squeeze past the Albères hills, reaching the sea at **Collioure**, a little seashore town (see p. 190) of immense charm, though too crowded with visitors. Collioure's Majorcan 'Royal Castle' rises from the very edge of the water, as does its unusual lighthouse, which is part of the church.

South from Collioure, the mountains close in upon the coast, narrowing the land until only a winding cliff road, with superb views, has space to pass from France into Spain. This, the most breathtaking part of the whole Languedoc–Roussillon coastline, is called the Côte Vermeille (difficult to translate exactly; it sounds odd in English — roughly, 'the Vermilion-tinted Coast') (see p. 190). Beyond Collioure only a handful of small places, all pleasant for a visit, remain before the frontier. The lively marina **Port-Vendres**, once the Romans' Portus-Veneris, the Port of Venus, later fortified by Vauban, has been largely rebuilt since 1944. Next, with rolling hillside vineyards around its pretty bay,

comes **Banyuls** (pronounce the 's' clearly), which produces, among others, some intriguing sweet fortified wines. Finally, the village of **Cerbère** marks the frontier with Spain — but the Catalan flag flies on both sides of the border. (See p. 188 for the Roussillon coast in more detail.)

The heart and soul of French Catalonia lies in the mountains, the Pyrenean forests and pastures south-west of Perpignan. The Canigou Massif, about 30km from Perpignan, dominates the lower mountains. Rising much higher than the surrounding peaks, it can be seen from a considerable distance in almost any direction. The Canigou heights separate Roussillon's two main river valleys, the Têt to its north and the Tech (pronounced Tek) to the south. Fertile and productive, these two rivers give Roussillon much of its agricultural wealth. With spring and autumn rains, a long dry summer and frost-free winter, the region provides the rest of France's population, so anxious to avoid produce which has been imported from abroad or ripened in storage, with freshly picked fruit and green vegetables at unseasonable times of year. Richly laden orchards of peach, nectarine, apricot and cherry — gorgeous with blossom in early spring — fill the lower Têt and Tech valleys.

Few roads connect the two rivers apart from the twisting D618 which approximately joins Ille-sur-Têt to Amélie-les-Bains. A useful road connecting the coast to the Têt, and by-passing the Perpignan sprawl, is the D615/D612, which runs from Ille-sur-Têt to Elne via Thuir. Travellers approaching from the north on their way to the Tech valley can also avoid Perpignan if they wish by passing through Rivesaltes on D615 to Pézilla-la-Rivière, then minor roads to Thuir, whence picturesque D615 to Céret on the Tech. The attractive old town of **Thuir**, with its maze of narrow lanes and squares, is noted for the production of apéritifs and liqueurs, especially Byrrh. In its church there is a Virgin and Child dating from about 1200, made of pewter. If you are passing through Thuir, it is worthwhile making the short journey, 6km along D48, to the handsome fortified village of **Castelnou**, watched over by a 10th-century keep. Beyond, D48 continues into an area of picturesque hills and typical little Catalan farm villages.

The more usual approach to the Tech valley is through **le Boulou**, small crossroads town (note unusual Romanesque portal of church) on autoroute A9 and route nationale N9. The N9 is the old highway which follows the valley of the river Rome up through the Albères heights to the Spanish border, passing through a series of fortified *cluses* (i.e. where a river valley narrows tightly) up to frontier village **le Perthus**. On the way up, fragments of the Romans' Via Domitia can be seen in the aptly-named Rome valley. Le Perthus was Hannibal's entry point into Gaul, and Via Domitia the road his elephants and his troops marched along. (The Roman highway descended from the Col du Perthus to the Tech valley, continuing across to Elne, up to Castel-Roussillon, rejoining the route of the present N9 at the Fort de Salses.)

Venturing south-west from le Boulou into the real mountains, D115 follows the Tech valley as it rises steeply from the plain up to its source on the Spanish border. The road soon crosses an early 14th-century bridge, locally known (as such old bridges so often are in Languedoc and Roussillon) as le Pont du Diable, the Devil's Bridge. Adjacent to it, off the main road, is the agreeable little old town of **Céret**, which, like Collioure on the coast, was a favourite spot with many great modern artists including Picasso and Braque; in the 1910s Céret was regarded as the 'Capital of Cubism'. There is a surprising Museum of Modern Art in the town with several Cubist paintings; there's a Picasso collection, and works by Chagall, Dali, Miró, Matisse and Juan Gris, as well as the Catalan sculptor Manolo (1872–1945): for it was to visit him, and the composer Déodat de Séverac (1873–1921) who lived here at the same time, that so many leading artists originally came to Céret. Aristide Maillol, the sculptor from nearby Banyuls, made a war memorial for the town.

Céret is proudly Catalan, with a Catalan Cultural Centre in place Pablo Picasso, regular open-air Sardana dancing, and also bullfighting; early in the year there is a Carnival (Shrove Tuesday), at Easter there is a colourful traditional procession and in August a big Sardana Festival. The *vieille ville*, with its ancient fortified gateways and broad tree-shaded interconnecting esplanades — place Pablo Picasso, place de la Liberté and place des Tilleuls — is especially likeable. The farms and orchards of Céret also happen to be well known in France for producing the very first cherries of the year: they are deliciously ripe by mid-April.

With views of the Roc de France summit (1450m) to the left and the ruined castle of hillside Palada on the right, D115 continues towards **Amélie-les-Bains**, formerly Arles-les-Bains, one of a number of small, ancient Pyrenean spas which were known to the Romans and enjoyed a period of vogue in the 19th century. Amélie has a score of different sulphur and sodium springs, and there is a fragment of Roman paving in a restored bathing pool. There's picturesque country round about, too, either for walking or driving, especially the Vallée du Mondony and the journey to the hilltop village of Montbolo. **Arles-sur-Tech**, the next town along, is the little 'capital' of the Vallespir district. A remote but devout religious community for centuries, Arles grew up around an important Benedictine abbey established here in the year 900. An interesting Romanesque abbey church of 1046, reconstructed in 1157, and its Gothic 13th-century cloisters, survive. Outside the church is a 4th-century white marble sarcophagus, known only as the Sainte Tombe, or Holy Tomb, from which seep a few drops a year of a strange clear liquid which (so the credulous locals would have it) defies chemical analysis. Above the sarcophagus a funerary effigy of a knight dates from the early 13th century. Above the church door, an early 11th-century Romanesque tympanum shows Christ in Glory in a Greek cross. The interior too is unusual-looking, unexpectedly high, and contains the tombs of 'saints' Abdon and Senned whose remains (already centuries old) were brought here in about the year 1000. In reality two martyred Kurdish Princes, Abdon and Senned were for some reason revered in Roussillon during the Dark Ages, and the presence of their bodies here was credited with protecting the villagers from the wolves and bears which roamed the mountains in those days. If you happen to be here between the 29th and 31st of July, you may see the annual procession in which the relics of the two men are carried around the village and water from the Sainte Tombe is distributed. In another side chapel are the three Crucifixion 'misteris' which are carried by Pénitents in their nocturnal Good Friday procession.

Arles gives easy access to some attractive mountain country, with marvellous opportunities for short excursions either on foot or by car. Particularly worth the effort is the walk, about 2 hours there and back, on easy paths, to the delightful Gorges de la Fou, about 100m deep but never more than 3m wide. There are many interesting little mountain villages to seek out nearby, several with unusual Romanesque churches. Not far beyond Arles, for example, D3 leads off south to **St. Laurent-de-Cerdans**, a striking-looking village, noted for its espadrilles incidentally, and farther along to **Coustouges**, a tiny place with a remarkable, lovely fortified 12th-century church, and eventually to the end of the road at Can Damoun, from which point the views into Spain reach as far as the Costa Brava. Another small turning (take D64 from la Forge del Mitg, near St. Laurent-de-Cerdans) goes to rustic **Serralongue**, with another old Romanesque church, and on the hill above, a 'conjurador' where traditionally the priest would — reverting to tried and tested pre-Christian incantations — attempt to control the weather at harvest time! Beyond Serralongue, the scenic minor route D44 leads up to remote **Lamanère**, the little-visited mountain village at the end of the road, most southerly *commune* in France.

The main road from Arles, D115, carries on up the Tech to reach **Prats-de-Mollo** (pop: only 1200), a steep little mountain town of considerable charm, securely enclosed by Vauban's fortifications. Prats (it means 'meadows' in Catalan), which hardly extends outside these 17th-century ramparts even today, divides naturally into a Ville Basse and the higher Ville d'Amoun. Narrow lanes and steps lead from one to the other. The large and unusual church in the lower town was mainly built in the 17th century, in Gothic style, on the site of a much older Romanesque building, the belfry of which survives in the present structure. Centre of the upper town is the Maison des Rois d'Aragon, supposedly a former hunting lodge of the Aragon kings. Nowadays Prats has become something of a resort for walkers in summer and cross-country skiers in winter. The surrounding summits are bristling with medieval watchtowers and fortifications.

Prats-de-Mollo is almost but not quite at the top of the Tech valley road: D115ᴬ climbs still higher towards the small spa **la Preste**, behind which are the Pic de Costabonne (2465m), and the source of the Tech. D115, veering south by twists and turns, works its way up to the Spanish border 14km away.

By contrast with the D115 and the Tech valley, the N116 which follows the river Têt up into the mountains is a major road taking quite a lot of traffic. It connects Perpignan with Andorra and Ax-les-Thermes. Where it has to squeeze through small old village centres, both the traffic and the villages suffer the effects. But in other places the road is broad and modern, sweeping around the high valley in easy turns

A capital in the Romanesque church of Serrabone priory

with superb mountain views. From the very start it runs through a succession of small places with marvellously Catalan-sounding names like St. Félieu-d'Avall and St. Félieu-d'Amont (Amont means 'upriver', Avall 'downriver'). Typically Catalan towers and churches rise above the modest village centres. Some, like **Ille-sur-Têt**, have a few last remnants of the fortifications once essential in this disputed territory. Just after Ille, at **Bouleternère**, a narrow lane winds up a river gorge to the lonely Augustinian priory of Serrabone, where the Romanesque church (11th century) has some fine capitals.

The main road presses on to **Prades**, ancient capital of the Conflent area. Though at the foot of high mountains, and right below the looming presence of the Canigou Massif, Prades is delightfully warm and Mediterranean. With its narrow lanes and notices in Catalan, it has plenty of atmosphere. The town's Gothic church is rather like Perpignan cathedral in miniature, the same hall-like interior lined with gaudy side chapels and fantastically exaggerated gilded retables, while the exterior, though made with rounded stones in a pattern, is strangely unadorned. The Spanish Catalan cellist Pablo Casals (1876–1973) chose Prades as his new home when he fled from Franco's Spain, and he established an annual festival of classical music here which now takes place 3km away at one of Roussillon's superb Romanesque abbeys: St Michel-de-Cuxa (or Sant Miquel del Cuxa).

This evocative and rambling old abbey, built of gorgeous warm-hued stone, stands right beside the road (D27) in a sunny wooded setting. Originally Benedictine, founded about the year 900 and largely rebuilt in the 11th century, it now houses a Cistercian community. An entrance fee is charged to look inside. However, the interior shockingly reveals the damage inflicted over the years. It was burned by Revolutionaries, and the Cloisters Museum in New York removed some of the best Romanesque capitals. The abbey church has unusual horseshoe-shaped (Mozarabic) arches. The abbey makes a fine setting for Casals' summer music festival.

This area has its share of small spa resorts; just north of Prades is **Molitg-les-Bains**, where the thermal baths are peacefully located in wooded country beside the Castellane river, while south of Prades, a little beyond St. Michel-de-Cuxa on the very slopes of Canigou, **Vernet-les-Bains** was a health resort popular among the English at the turn of the century. Rudyard Kipling, for example, came here regularly as did Hilaire Belloc, who described Canigou as 'the mountain which many men who have hardly heard the name have been looking for all their lives'. Presumably Vernet's English visitors used to go together every Sunday to the Anglican Church of St. George which I was amazed to discover here. According to an inscription, the foundation stone was laid in 1911 by no less a personage than Lord Roberts. A sign on the church says that although it still belongs to The United Society for the Propagation of the Gospel, it has been given on permanent loan to the Catholic Church on condition that Anglican services be performed here 'as and when judged necessary'. This curious arrangement, if I understood the sign correctly, has been agreed between the Bishop of Fulham and Gibraltar (*is* there such a diocese?) and the Bishop of Perpignan.

Vernet makes an ideal starting point for a walk to the top of the **Pic du Canigou** (2784m). There are two main routes, one on foot all the way, direct from Vernet, the other a difficult driveable track which starts on the Vernet–Prades road and goes to the Chalet-Hôtel des Cortalet at 2,150m, after which there's still a 2-hour climb to the summit. Going up the Canigou is serious walking, steep and in places difficult, so proper boots and waterproof clothing are recommended. From the top, which you may not have to yourself, the view of the eastern Pyrenees is incomparable, and

Festivals and Events in French Catalonia

February: Carnivals and Village Festivals

Carnivals at CÉRET, PERPIGNAN, ARGELÈS and VINÇA, and traditional Fêtes de l'Ours (Bear Festivals) at PRATS-DE-MOLLO and ST. LAURENT-DE-CERDANS.

Easter Processions

On the night of Good Friday: PERPIGNAN — Procession de la Sanch (see p. 150); ARLES-SUR-TECH, BOULETERNÈRE and COLLIOURE — Processions of black-robed Penitent Brotherhoods. *Easter Sunday*: CÉRET and ILLE-SUR-TÊT — Procession of the Resurrection; traditional chanting in the streets of other towns and villages.

Midsummer ('Fête de St. Jean')

23rd June — bonfires and celebrations include fires on the summit of CANIGOU and other peaks, and traditional celebrations in PERPIGNAN; *24th–25th June* — Fires and festivities at AMÉLIE-LES-BAINS.

July and August

PRADES — Pablo Casals Music Festival, end July/beginning August, Classical music in the nearby Abbey of St. Michel-de-Cuxa; CÉRET — Sardana Festival, usually 3rd Sunday in August, hundreds of skilled dancers in traditional dress.

18th–21st September

CÉRET — Fête de St. Ferréol: folk dances, bullfights, religious ceremonies.

Christmas

PERPIGNAN, CÉRET and PRATS-DE-MOLLO — traditional chanting 'dels Goigs'.

although everything in between may be lost in haze one can often see right across Languedoc to the Cévennes, while the Costa Brava is visible to the south-east. When Hilaire Belloc stood up here, he was able to see 'a plain like an inlaid work of chosen stones; and, in a curve, all that coast which at the close of the Roman Empire was, perhaps, the wealthiest in Europe'.

Canigou is regarded with feelings akin to awe by Catalans, at least by those on the French side, who consider it as somehow symbolic of their nationhood. Often half-hidden by mists, the bleak solitary peak does

Overleaf: *The Abbey of St. Michel-de-Cuxa*

present an alluring, enticing sight. People fascinated by its aura of mystery must have been climbing the mountain for centuries, and it remains a popular goal for walkers, so King Pedro III of Aragón's claim to have been the first person ever to reach its summit (in 1285) has long been humoured as a piece of royal nonsense. In any case, it might have been treason to challenge him, particularly since he announced that at the top of Canigou there was a dragon living in a lake. Certainly he was quite mistaken about the lake, but as for the dragon, I don't know.

High on the slope of Canigou, isolated and hidden among the rocky crags, yet another fine Romanesque abbey, St. Martin-de-Canigou, once provided as silent and ascetic a retreat from the world as could be found anywhere. It has a simple, sturdy, modest grace and dates from the year 1007, when the monastery was founded by a repentant father, Count Giufred of Cerdagne, who had killed his son; he did some of the building work himself, and lived out the rest of his life here. Although restored and altered in this century, St. Martin retains much that dates from those early days, including the capitals of the exquisite cloisters and garden. Below the Abbey church is an older structure, the dark 10th-century chapel called Notre-Dame-sous-Terre. Although the climb is extremely steep, and takes at least half an hour each way, the Abbey is by no means impossible to reach. There is a proper footpath all the way to it from just above the village of Casteil, 3km from Vernet-les-Bains. Indeed, the walk, through lovely woods occasionally breaking to give superb mountain views, is perhaps the best part of a visit to the Abbey. Arrival at the building

Traditional wrought-iron shop signs in Villefranche-de-Conflent

itself can even be a little unsatisfying if, as happened when I went there, there is a noisy party of tourists milling about in this otherwise tranquil spot. Just below the abbey, standing to one side of the pathway, you will pass a curious small building popularly known as St. Martin-le-Vieux. Undated, possibly pre-Romanesque, this little chapel was rebuilt from its ruins in 1977. One theory is that it may have been the ossuary of the monastic community. It provides a welcome pause from the relentless climb, and it's well worth stopping here for a moment if only to take in the magnificent view from a terrace behind the chapel.

Return to the N116 either by going back through Vernet, or by following the pretty lanes (D116, D6) via the picturesque village of **Sahorre** (attractive old Romanesque church). Both routes reach the Têt valley again at the impressively fortified little town, really hardly more than a village, of **Ville-franche-de-Conflent**. No traffic is permitted to enter the town gates, within which the streets are paved with marble flagstones and lined with medieval buildings. Many of those which are now shops display remarkable wrought iron signs, a local tradition. The rough pinkish marble, seen everywhere in Villefranche, is locally quarried — and the town's intriguing church of St. Jacques, hard by the ramparts and main gate, is more or less made of it. Fronted by a charming square with a few well-placed café tables, the 11th- to 13th-century church has a distinctive Romanesque tower, while inside the building are several striking ensembles of naïve statuary illustrating biblical scenes. It's worth having a good look around Villefranche; the place is like a living museum piece. Side alleys run down to the river Cady which meets the Têt just here. The ramparts, originally 16th-century Aragonese, underwent the usual restructuring and modification

Le Petit Train Jaune

One of Roussillon's most delightful amenities is the Petit Train Jaune, the Little Yellow Train, which runs from Villefranche-de-Conflent up to Enveigt/La Tour de Carol (where it connects with the main line to Paris). The total distance is 63km, the highest point of the journey being the station at Bolquère/Eyne (1579m). Just a two-carriage country train like many another in France, this one is painted in cheery yellow and red, and has somehow acquired a sort of eccentric charm. It passes through wild and spectacular mountain country, and calls at small rustic stations where at times it must be hailed like a bus. In summer, open carriages make the journey even more enjoyable. Apart from providing an essential transport service to the villagers, it is especially useful to walkers, who take the train to one station and walk across country to another. As car drivers climb the Têt valley on the N116, the railway line appears and reappears, most noticeably where it crosses some remarkable viaducts.

Phone 68.35.50.50 for more information.

after Vauban had inspected them in 1665 following the French takeover of Roussillon. Part of the fortification is formed by a Citadel, while from an adjacent hilltop ruins of an older fortress still stand guard.

It's an easy drive as the highway, wider here, lazily skirts the mountainsides all the way from Villefranche to **Mont-Louis**. This simple village is another erstwhile frontier fortress, protected by imposing double ramparts entered through a superb main gateway. An ancient fortified village, it was specially recreated as a garrison town by Vauban in 1679–1681, and remains one to this day. There does seem something incongruous and yet also very fitting in the sight of young soldiers in modern combat gear — sometimes behind the wheel of a big army truck — going in and out of the 300-year-old walls of this town with its nearby snow-covered peaks. Inevitably it brings to mind thoughts on the continuing urge for national defence, and the changing frontiers and alliances within Europe, as the centuries have passed. An even greater incongruity, perhaps, which Mont-Louis offers for the contemplation of passing travellers is the sight, beside the ramparts, of the curious curved mirrors of one of the world's first operational solar energy power plants. The village makes a good centre for exploring, whether on footpaths or country lanes. There's plenty to see nearby; for example, nearby **Planès** has a strange Romanesque church, dating from the 11th century and built to a unique triangular pattern.

The remote Abbey of St. Martin-du-Canigou

Mont-Louis is a crossroads. The river Têt veers away north-west towards the heights of Pic Carlit (2921m), Roussillon's tallest peak; the valley can be followed into the wooded mountains as far as Lake Bouillouses on steep minor road D60. D118 heads north from the town over the broad valley floor of the Capcir, a spacious airy countryside enclosed by walls of mountain on each side. All this is fine walking country. GR footpaths with their familiar red and white markers ramble among these wild, wooded hills and clean cool lakes. Villages and hamlets are extremely rustic, until recently very isolated, retaining a simple pastoral way of life; local people speak Catalan. Where the Capcir reaches the border of the Aude département, the road leaves Roussillon and enters Languedoc: the ruined Cathar fortress of Quérigut lies just across the line. A hair-raisingly steep and difficult narrow mountain road — with serious risk of avalanche and sudden heavy snowfalls — connects the Capcir, via Quérigut, to Ax-les-Thermes (p. 128). Perhaps picturesque in clear weather, when I took this road on a June morning, dense swirling mist and snow all but hid the precipitous edge of the broken and potholed roadway as it threaded cautiously along sheer mountainside. I met not a single car in 30km — locals, I guessed, have more sense than to take this road!

Continuing south-west from Mont-Louis towards the Spanish border, the road splits into two, skirting either side of the large Spanish enclave of **Llivia** and its surrounding country.

N116 goes south of the enclave, along the edge of forested mountains with some excellent walks. **Saillagouse**,

6km from Mont-Louis, makes a good starting point for visits by foot or car to well-sited villages like **Llo** or **Eyne**, and the meadows and pastures beside the narrow gorge of the river Sègre. Following a footpath up the Sègre all the way to the Col de Llo, I discovered in open pasture on the very frontier with Spain a herd of huge half-wild horses wearing cowbells. Obviously being raised as cattle, it turned out that these enormous creatures were originally bred as cavalry horses and now are 'chevals de boucherie', left to care for themselves in the mountains until the farmer wants to catch one for the slaughterhouse. 'A very cheap and easy form of farming', as a local farmer explained.

Beyond Saillagouse, N116 goes on to the Spanish border at **Bourg-Madame** and, on the other side, Puigcerdà. Alternatively, near Saillagouse, take a small right turn, D33, into the Spanish enclave, which makes a fascinating visit. On reaching the unmanned customs post with its No Entry sign, press on regardless; I have crossed this little frontier on several occasions without ever encountering a *douanier*. Visitors are welcome in Catalan-speaking Llivia, ancient capital of the Cerdagne. Unsightly modern apartment blocks on the outskirts of the old town give a misleading impression. Turn off the main through road to enter a labyrinth of narrow, steep medieval streets. At the village centre is a fortified church and an interesting 15th-century pharmacy now preserved as a museum (next to tourist office).

At Bourg-Madame, N116 meets the major N20 highway. Turn here to go a few kilometres north, to the village of Ur, where D618 heads away east again, and returns to Mont-Louis on the

Flora and Fauna of High Roussillon

There is an astonishing abundance and variety of wild flowers on the slopes of the eastern Pyrenees. High mountain meadows can be seen all summer long bursting with delicate blooms, mingling familiar buttercups and daisies with gentians, lilies, lupins and, in both spring and autumn, millions of crocuses. Open ground is matted with fragrant wild herbs, especially several kinds of thyme, while in the shelter of the woods grow dozens of sorts of mushrooms, edible and otherwise.

Animals still plentiful in the Roussillon mountains include the *sanglier*, the fast and furious wild boar; the izard, which is what the people of the Pyrenees call a chamois (maintaining that there is a difference between the two); the mouflon, the wild forerunner of the domestic sheep, and said to be the easiest to see of all the region's wild animals; the genet cat, like a bad-tempered kitten in a leopard skin; and the marmot, what Americans call a woodchuck, a big cuddly cousin of the rat.

north side of the Spanish enclave. N20 carries on north from Ur, climbing through high pleasant farm country beside the river Carol up to Col de Puymorens. After the Col the road leaves Catalonia and quickly spirals down to enter the Aude département, soon reaching Ax-les-Thermes (p. 128).

The Story of Llivia

Llivia, once a Roman town called Julia Livia, capital of the Cerdagne, was still the most important town in this part of the Pyrenees at the time of the 1659 Treaty which was intended to transfer all Spanish territories on the mountains' north slopes to France. The treaty did not specify exactly where the new frontier should be drawn, but stated that 33 villages must pass from Spanish to French rule. In practice it was planned that, as far as possible, the border would follow the watershed dividing the rivers which flowed into France from those which flowed into Spain. However, the people of Llivia objected, not only to the way in which Catalonia was about to be divided into two, and not only to becoming French, but most of all to the classification of their historic town as one of '33 villages'. They fought their inclusion in the treaty on the grounds that Llivia was not a village. And to further support their case they pointed out that although the river Sègre, which runs through Llivia, emerges from a spring on the north slope of the Pic de Sègre, it in fact turns full circle and flows into Spain. Their arguments allowed the commune of Llivia and its surrounding pastures to remain 'temporarily' as a Spanish enclave inside France. Over 300 years later the enclave is still there.

Mirrors of the Four Solaire *('solar oven') beside the Pyrenean village of Odeillo*

D618 rises and turns to skirt the **Targassonne** area, with its weird glacial rock formations and (just off the road to the left) its solar power station (no longer open to visitors), before descending into the resort of **Font-Romeu**. Built almost entirely since the 1910s, there's not much to Font-Romeu except hotels and holiday apartments, mainly geared to cross-country skiers and summer walkers. Yet it's not unattractive thanks to its arcaded pavements and fortunate setting, looking out across the Cerdagne plateau. The French Winter Olympics training takes place here in a marvellous sports complex which is open to the public. Although the resort is entirely modern, Font-Romeu takes its name from the Foun Roumeú (Catalan for 'Pilgrim Spring') at the adjacent **Ermitage**. Here, in a 17th-century chapel, with a magnificent retable (by

Joseph Sunyer, 1707) and with the 'miraculous' spring itself in the wall, is housed a mysterious Black Virgin, called La Vierge de l'Invention. The legend surrounding her is that the statue was discovered — 'invented' — by a bull which, scratching at the soil near an ancient sacred spring, prompted its owner to dig into the ground where he unearthed the Virgin. Perhaps in honour of the bull's own annual routine, the statue spends the summer grazing months in the church at Ermitage, and the winter season lower down the mountain in the lovely old Romanesque church (note the lovely porch) at **Odeillo**.

The processions to remove the Virgin from one site to another are major events in the calendar of the devout peasants of the area. On the 8th of September is the Aplech del Baixar (the Festival of the Descent), when a

Solar Energy in the Pyrenees

Thanks to exceptionally clean air and a higher total of sunshine hours per year than anywhere else in France, the eastern Pyrenees provide the best possible environment for generating energy from sunlight. The area was in the forefront of research into this field, with early experiments at Mont-Louis in the 1950s, and the establishing of a solar power station (Thémis) at Targassonne in 1982. At Thémis, salt is used to store heat, and it is kept at a constant 400°C. France now regards solar power stations as a technology export rather than an energy source for domestic use, and develops projects similar to Thémis for poorer countries which need cheap energy. At Odeillo the French have taken the lead in another direction by constructing the world's most powerful 'solar oven'. Using concave mirrors, sunlight is concentrated into the centre of an enclosed crucible or oven. The heating power is equivalent to 1,000kW, and the oven temperature reaches 4,000°C. This is used by commercial organisations to treat materials, and by research institutes, including NASA, to test the effects of ultra-high temperatures.

solemn gathering of local people transports the statue down the 3km path to Odeillo. On Trinity Sunday (June), the Aplech del Pujar, she is carried back up to the summer resting place.

The church at Odeillo, with its aura of unfathomable age and dark superstition, is just a few minutes' stroll from the world's most powerful solar energy plant (*'four solaire'*, or solar oven) which, with devastating simplicity, consists of one vast concave mirror facing a great assembly of smaller mirrors which reflect the sunlight. The mirrors move like bizarre high-tech sunflowers to follow the course of the sun across the sky. Inside the building on the site there is a continuous free

exhibition with video explaining the workings of the solar oven.

Odeillo's juxtaposition of 12th-century Romanesque with 20th-century solar, both as vibrantly alive as each other, together with the ski chalets at Font-Romeu, seems to capture the essence of French Catalonia. The D618 from Font-Romeu back to Mont-Louis, giving wide views across the plateau and mountains, is fittingly called the *Balcon de Cerdagne*.

For the Roussillon coast (Canet-Plage, St. Cyprien, Argelès-Plage, Collioure, Port-Ventres, Banyuls) see Chapter 8: The Coast.

Hotels and Restaurants

LES ANGLES: **Hôtel Yaka** (68.04.46.46), outside village, overlooking Lake Matemale in the Capcir, clean, comfortable modern hotel, moderate prices.

ARGELÈS-SUR-MER: **Le Cottage**, 21 rue Arthur Rimbaud (68.81.07.33), straightforward, quiet, modestly priced 2-star Logis.

LE BOULOU: **Relais des Chartreuses**, Les Chartreuse (68.83.15.88), good hotel and restaurant in tranquil rural setting, stylish and comfortable, quite pricey.

CASTELNOU: **L'Hostal restaurant** (68.53.45.42), excellent unpretentious village restaurant, good food, reasonable prices.

CÉRET: **La Terrasse au Soleil**, very good hotel–restaurant in lovely setting, not cheap.

FONT-ROMEU: **Hôtel Carlit** (68.30.07.45), large, popular, comfortable hotel with moderately priced restaurant.

MOLITG-LES-BAINS: **Château de Riell** (68.05.04.40), luxurious Relais et Châteaux hotel and first-class restaurant in superb location, very expensive.

PERPIGNAN: **Hôtel Athena**, 1 rue Queya (68.34.37.63), modest, quiet, inexpensive, central.
Park Hôtel and Chapon Fin restaurant 18 bd J. Bourrat (68.35.14.14), modern, comfortable, with excellent restaurant (not cheap).
Hôtel de la Loge, 1 rue Fabrice-Nabot (68.34.54.84), central, comfortable.
Restaurant François Villon, 1 rue Four St. Jean (68.51.18.43), excellent restaurant, impressive setting, reasonable price.

SAILLAGOUSE: **Hôtel Planes** ('Maison Cerdane'), pl de Cerdagne (68.04.72.08), popular, inexpensive village hotel with very good, reasonably priced restaurant.

VILLEFRANCHE-DE-CONFLENT: **Au Grill** 81 rue St. Jean (68.96.17.65), best little eating place in town, inexpensive.

Hotel Bookings Service

Centrale de Réservations Pyrénées–Roussillon, C.D.T., BP 540, 66005 Perpignan Cedex. Phone: 68.34.29.94 poste 5. Telex: 500776. Up-to-date information on availability of hotel rooms, campsites, etc.; reservations made.

Museums

ARGELÈS-SUR-MER: See Chapter 8: The Coast, p. 171.

On Pic du CANIGOU: **Abbaye de St. Martin-de-Canigou**, ¹/₂-hr from Casteil, (68.05.50.03). Fine 11th-12th-century monastic buildings. *Open daily.*

CÉRET: **Casa Catalana de la Cultura**: pl Pablo Picasso (68.87.00.36) for information). *June–Sep: daily (exc Sun, Tue, fêtes) 10–12, 2–6; Oct–May: daily (exc Tue & fêtes) 2–6.*
Musée d'Art Moderne (Museum of Modern Art) (68.87.00.36 for information). Includes Picasso, Braque, Dufy, Chagall. *Jul–Aug: daily (exc Tue) 10–12, 3–7; rest of year: daily (exc Tue and fêtes) 10–12, 3–5.*

COLLIOURE: see Chapter 8: The Coast, p. 171.

ELNE: **Cathedral and Cloisters** (68.22.05.38). *Jul–Aug: daily (exc Tue) 10–12, 2–4.45; rest of year: daily (exc Sun) 10–12, 2–4.45.*

ODEILLO: **Solar Oven (Four Solaire)** (68.30.10.24). *Exterior and exhibition room only daily 9–5.*

PERPIGNAN: **Musée d'Arts et Traditions Populaires du Roussillon ('Casa Païral')**: inside 15th-century fortified gatehouse Le Castillet (68. 35. 66. 30 for information). Catalan folk museum. *Daily exc Tue and some fêtes. 15th Jun–15th Sep: 9.30–12, 2.30–7; 16th Sep–14th Jun: 9–12, 2–6.*
Musée Rigaud: 16 rue de l'Ange (68. 35. 66. 30). Fine arts museum, esp Rigaud and 14th–16th-century Primitive Catalan collections. *Daily exc Tue and some fêtes. 15th Jun–15th Sep: 9.30–12, 2.30–7; 16th Sep–14th Jun: 9–12, 2–6.*
Palais des Rois de Majorque (Palace of Majorcan Kings): inside Citadel. *Daily exc Tue and some fêtes. 15th Jun–15th Sep: 9.30–12, 2.30–7; 16th Sep–14th Jun: 9–12, 2–6.*

PRADES: **Abbaye St. Michel-de-Cuxa**: 3km south of Prades (68.05.02.40). *Daily exc Tue.*
Musée Pablo Casals: rue Victor Hugo (68.96.20.91). *Summer: daily (exc Sat pm & Sun) 9–12, 3–6; out of season: Tue only 9–12.*

ST. LAURENT-DE-CERDANS: **Museum of Espadrilles** (68.39.50.06). *May–Sep: daily (exc Tue) 9–12, 3–7.*

SALSES: **Fort de Salses**: Vast 15th–16th-century fortress. Guided tours only (1hr). *1st Apr–30th Sep: 10–11; 1st Oct–31st Mar: 2–4. Closed Tue in summer, Wed rest of year, and some fêtes.*

TAUTAVEL: **Musée de la Préhistoire**: la Tour-de-France (68.29.07.76). Interesting display concerning 'Tautavel Man', based on the discovery of a 450,000-year-old skull here. *10–12, 2–6.*

THUIR : **El Celler** or **Le Cellier**: Museum of local vineyards and wine. *Call 68.06.45.86 for opening times.*
Byrrh Distilleries (68.53.05.42). Visits and tastings. *Apr–Sep: daily (exc Sun) 8.30– 11.45, 2.30–5.45; Mar & Oct: Mon–Fri 8.30–11.45, 2.30–5.45; rest of year: by arrangement. Closed Sun, 1 May, & 7 Oct.*

Tourist Offices

CRT offices (regional information): 12 rue Foch, 34000 Montpellier (67.60.55.42). CDT Offices (information on the département): Palais Consulaire, quai de Lattre-de-Tassigny, 66005 Perpignan (68.34.29.94/68.34.29.95); also at Maison des Pyrénées, 15 rue St. Augustin, 75009 Paris (42.61.58.18).
OTSI offices (local information): AMÉLIE-LES-BAINS: pl de la République (68.39.01.98); ARGELÈS-SUR-MER: pl des Arènes (68.81.15.85); LE BOULOU: pl de la Mairie (68.83.15.60); CERBÈRE: 1 av de la Côte Vermeille (68.88.42.36); CÉRET: Av G. Clemenceau (68.87.00.58); FONT-ROMEU: Av E. Brousse (68.30.02.74); MOLITG-LES-BAINS (68.96.27.58); MONT-LOUIS (68.04.21.97); PERPIGNAN: Quai de Lattre-de-Tassigny (68.34.29.94); PRATS-DE-MOLLO: Foyer Rural, pl Le Firal (68.39.70.83); SAILLAGOUSE: in high season only at la Mairie (68.04.72.89); SALSES: 13 pl St. Jacques (68.38.66.13); VERNET-LES-BAINS: 1 sq Mal-Joffre (68.05.55.35); VILLEFRANCHE-DE-CONFLENT: pl de la Mairie (68.96.10.78).

Where there is no tourist office, apply to the Town Hall (Mairie or Hôtel de Ville).

Sports and Leisure

SKIING: The Roussillon Pyrenees have good no-frills downhill skiing and over 200km of *ski de fond* and *ski Nordic* (cross country) trails. Main ski resorts are Font-Romeu, Les Angles (Matemale) and Pyrenees-2000. Best of the cross-country pistes are in the Capcir area. Information from Conféderation de la Neige Catalane, Maison du Tourisme, 66120 Font-Romeu (68.30.02.74); Club Alpin Français, 4 rue de l'Académie, 66000 Perpignan.

WALKING, HIKING: Main Grandes Randonnées (GR) footpaths in the region are GR10 and GR36. Good starting/finishing points are Saillagouse, Mont-Louis, Font-Romeu, Prades (for Canigou), Les Angles. Useful information from Maison du Tourisme in Perpignan; Club Alpin Français, 4 rue de l'Academie, 66000 Perpignan; Association des Randonnées, Pyrénéennes, 4 rue de Villefranche, 09200 St. Girons (61.66.02.19). Inn-Travel, Park Street, Hovingham, York YO6 4JZ (065 382 425), have inclusive package holidays for individual walkers in the Roussillon Pyrenees.

8
The Coast

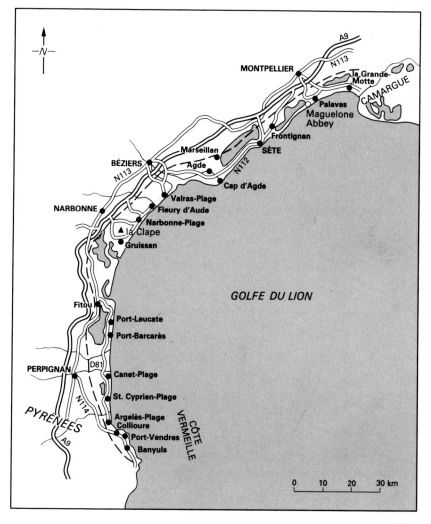

Languedoc and Roussillon have 200km of broad sandy beaches extending along the Mediterranean in an almost unbroken curve from the Spanish border to the Rhône. Unpolluted air and seawater, long dry summers, a rustic hinterland, and inland towns formed by twenty-five centuries of civilisation, heighten the appeal. Just behind the coastline a string of hazy *étangs*, shallow saltwater lagoons, separated from the sea by *lidos*, narrow ribbons of sand, run parallel to the sea and give the shore a dreamlike feeling of remoteness, a sense of being enveloped by sunshine and water, cut off from the real world. Beyond the *étangs*, a vast expanse of vineyards rolls away from the sea to the shimmering hills of the interior.

Yet until the early 1960s there was virtually nothing at all along most of this coastline except the old harbours at Sète and Collioure, and a few shabby little resort villages. It was an area strictly for its own enthusiasts, otherwise completely unknown and ignored. Then, in 1963, in a far-reaching effort to revive the economic prospects of this underdeveloped part of France, the Government set out to create a tourist industry for Languedoc.

Its first step was to build from scratch a number of new resorts. At the start only four were planned — a brand new town at la Grande-Motte to begin with, then the rebuilding of Carnon-Plage, next a new resort at Gruissan, then a fourth (later named Fleury d'Aude) at the mouth of the Aude. As work progressed, more were added to the list, until eventually there were nine resorts under construction. Each of them was to be built around a marina. Architecture was to be imaginative, without offending local traditions.

Facilities were to be ultra-modern but not out of reach of ordinary holiday-makers. Each resort was to have an individual style, a theme, a concept which it could develop and promote.

There were expensive problems to overcome, for example the lack of roads or other amenities. Worst of all was that the *étangs* were the prolific breeding ground of no fewer than 41 varieties of mosquito. A huge programme to eliminate the mosquito has been astonishingly successful (there are hardly any at all on this part of the Mediterranean). Now, Languedoc's *étangs* are more associated with gorgeous flocks of pink flamingos and other birdlife.

Over 25 years later, the success of the whole programme is not in doubt. What one thinks of the new resort towns themselves is a matter of opinion. If it is not easy to build a new town, it is even more difficult to give it a soul. On the whole, the purpose-built resorts suffer from the fact that they have no past and are not yet real, lived-in places. Yet the *aménagement* of Languedoc's coastline has undoubtedly been handled with care and sensitivity — it could hardly have been done better. Thousands of hectares of land have been reafforested; resorts are surrounded by greenery; each new town is encircled by a protected area where no building is allowed; to avoid polluting the sea (cleaner here than almost anywhere else in the Mediterranean) sophisticated waste treatment plants have been installed. Even the elimination of the mosquitoes was achieved with biodegradable products! And, as part of the operation, already existing resort villages, such as Palavas and Argelès, were also given substantial funds to improve facilities and

The New Resorts

Since the mid-1960s, construction or reconstruction has planted a total of ten marina-beach resorts along this once-deserted coastline ...

Port-Camargue (1970): on the Camargue coast near the ancient walled city of Aigues-Mortes; an imaginative marina with accommodation on islands;

La Grande-Motte (1966): strange pyramidal architecture, now with permanent population of over 5,000;

Carnon: resort adjoining Palavas, near Montpellier, it was rebuilt and revitalised as part of the coastal development programme;

Cap d'Agde (started 1970 — still not complete): most successful of the new holiday areas, best known for its vast Quartier Naturiste;

Fleury d'Aude (sporadic construction since 1967, still continuing): a green and relaxed smaller-scale development;

Gruissan (1973): at the foot of the Montagne de la Clape, near Narbonne, adjacent to an old fishing village, distinctive architecture;

Port-Leucate (1968 — unfinished): large marina-leisure port, with pleasant architecture, no high-rise building, tranquil atmosphere, with green paths, and naturist campsites, set between huge *étang* on one side and sea on the other;

Port-Barcarès (1968); lively resort with masses of watersports and other energetic leisure facilities;

Saint-Cyprien (started 1968 — construction continues): popular sporty 'St. Cyp' is well placed on a sandy beach with the Pyrenees close behind;

Argelès-Plage: old Roussillon resort vastly expanded and improved during the development programme. Specialising in camping, it has over 60 sites ranging from 2–4 stars, with space for over 13,000 tents.

smarten themselves up. The whole region has benefited from the investment plan. Even visitors who come specifically to explore the completely undeveloped areas of coast — and they are still extensive — are probably here partly because of the publicity and improved image occasioned by the development programme.

The first of the new towns, begun in 1966 on the flat and featureless shores of the western Camargue, was one of the most startling. Setting the tone of ambitious planning and audacious architecture, **la Grande-Motte**, designed by Jean Balladur, achieved instant fame or notoriety for its ziggurat-shaped or pyramidal apartment blocks. Dubbed 'futuristic' by commentators at the time, and still by some today, these buildings in fact now look rather dated. The principle behind them is that every floor has an unobstructed panoramic view. Having heard so much about the pyramids, what surprised me most was that a good deal of the town actually consists of buildings which look perfectly conventional. The surrounding landscape was extensively planted with greenery, irrigated by underground

La Grande-Motte, first of the Languedoc coast's new resorts

channels. The resort encourages gentle sports activity, offering first rate modern facilities with instruction for tennis, cycling, swimming and, especially, golf. In one way, la Grande-Motte has proved a great success, because it has attracted a permanent population of over 5,000.

East of la Grande-Motte lies the broad watery wilderness of the Camargue; within easy visiting distance are the small old resort of **le Grau-du-Roi**, new marina **Port-Camargue**, and the old walled medieval town of **Aigues-Mortes** ('dead waters'), stranded and immaculately preserved among the salty wastes. 'If it is dead,' said Henry James on seeing Aigues-Mortes, 'it is very neatly embalmed.'

To the west, fast main road D62 makes a straight run, along a narrow

strip of land between sea and *étang*, to **Carnon-Plage**. Carnon, close to Montpellier's Frejorges airport, merges into the older beach resort and fishing harbour **Palavas-les-Flots** (Palavas 'the waves'). In 1890, when Augustus Hare went to Palavas, he was struck by the 'picturesqueness' of its red balconies, green shutters and blue waters. Much of that charm had vanished without trace by the time I made my visit, almost one hundred years later. On the other hand, it still has more than neighbouring Carnon. Palavas remains as it has always been, the most popular beach for days out from Montpellier, only 9km away.

Interestingly, 4km farther along the beach from Palavas, all that remains of a much older, once populous seashore community at **Maguelone** is its fortified church, a former cathedral dating from 1178 (work had started on the building in 1110). More like a castle than a church, the exterior is defensive and largely unornamented, although the curious west doorway has unusual carving. The walls are massively thick. Among a cluster of cedar, eucalyptus and parasol pine, raised on slightly higher ground than the surrounding sands, the site is lost, lonely, peaceful and tragic. Until 1708, when the construction of the Rhône–Sète Canal cut straight through the causeway, Maguelone was connected by a small road (now D185ᴱ) directly to Ville-neuve-lès-Maguelone on the opposite side of the *étang*.

Maguelone's story started at least as long ago as the 2nd century, when there was already a Greek or Phoenician trading port here. It grew and prospered, became an episcopal centre, but was seized by the Saracens in the 8th century. It was quickly retaken by Charles Martel, who everywhere had notable successes against the Saracens, but he destroyed the town in case it should prove too difficult to defend against further Islamic attacks. Neighbouring Villeneuve was founded at that time. Unwilling to fade away, the community reappeared, with a new church which was rebuilt and fortified to become the building which survives today. It continued to thrive, but so did Montpellier, which eventually took Maguelone's place as the episcopal capital in the 16th century. It was the Wars of Religion which finished the town off finally: Maguelone (itself largely Protestant) was seized alternately by Catholic and Protestant forces, considerably damaged, its fortifications were

knocked down by Richelieu in 1622, and ultimately it was completely destroyed by Louis XIII's Catholic troops in 1633.

Beyond Maguelone there's no coast road. Palavas, Carnon and la Grande-Motte are linked to Montpellier by fast major roads; to move farther along the coast the best way is either to pass through Montpellier or, just as quick, take minor roads around the *étangs* towards Frontignan and Sète.

The environs of **Frontignan** are not pretty, although the town (or village) centre is not without some attractions. There is, for example, a fortified 12th-century church, and a number of fine 16th-century houses can be seen. But Frontignan is a highly industrialised port area noted above all for two things, and I sincerely hope there is no connection between them — refining oil, and making rich, sweet muscat wine. The wine, Muscat de Frontignan, praised by both Rabelais and Voltaire, is one of the best of Languedoc's excellent *vins doux naturels*, those curious fortified wines that taste almost like sherry. Even if you want to try it on its home ground, there is still no need

The lintel and tympanum of Maguelone cathedral, along the beach from Palavas

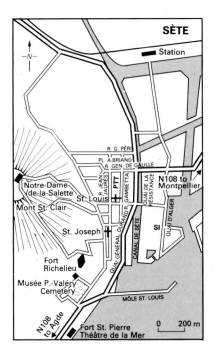

SÈTE

Station

Notre-Dame-de-la-Salette
Mont St. Clair
St. Louis
St. Joseph
Fort Richelieu
Musée P.-Valéry
Cemetery
MÔLE ST. LOUIS
Fort St. Pierre
Théâtre de la Mer
N108 to Agde
R. G. PÉRI
PL A.BRIAND
R GEN. DE GAULLE
R. JEAN JAURÈS
PTT
GAMBETTA
QUAI DE LA RÉSISTANCE
N108 to Montpellier
QUAI GÉNÉRAL DUGAN DR
CANAL DE SÈTE
SI
QUAI D'ALGER
0   200 m

Atlantic. Another important waterway enters Sète's large and complex harbour area from the other direction, the Rhône–Sète Canal, which links the town to Avignon and the Rhône. With such excellent waterway connections, it is not surprising that the town has prospered for centuries and continues to do so. Fishing has long been vitally important here, and now so too are related industries like fish processing and canning; but Sète also uses cheap, poorer quality wines, of which there are plenty round about, for making things like wine-vinegar and apéritifs.

Despite all the industry, and a lot of traffic, the town has enormous charm and a youthful atmosphere. The main waterfront area is along the two quays (really just the same one) on the canal's west side, Quai de la République and Quai Général-Dagobert, which run beside the Vieux-Port where scores of boats jostle picturesquely for space at the dockside. The excellent and totally unpretentious restaurants along here do not cater solely for tourists, incidentally: most of their customers, especially at lunchtime, are the *Sétois* themselves. From the port, the quiet rue Général de Gaulle heads up the hill, past a pleasant square (place Léon Blum), intersecting the narrow and bustling main shopping streets (rues Gambetta and Jean Jaurès) with their smart boutiques and fine food specialists. The pâtisseries sell brioche-like cakes and breads, traditional in Sète. Rue Jean Jaurès, changing its name a couple of times on the way, passes the 17th-century church of St. Louis, and climbs in turn past Fort Richelieu; a local museum (Musée Paul-Valéry) with exhibits on Paul Valéry, Georges Brassens, water jousting and the Canal

to linger in Frontignan, for **Sète** (pop: 40,500), right next door, is bristling with agreeable restaurants and café-bars.

Sète covers the lower slopes of Mont St. Clair, a surprisingly steep little hill (175m) which rises abruptly between sea and *étang*. The emblem of the town is a dolphin, 'because', locals unconvincingly told me, 'that is what Mont St. Clair looks like.' I could not quite see this myself, but then, neither is there much resemblance between Sète's fishy heraldic creature and a real dolphin. At the foot of the hill, a lively and attractive quayside, lined with popular seafood restaurants, fronts onto the Canal de Sète, part of the Canal du Midi which connects Sète and the Mediterranean with the river Garonne, Toulouse, Bordeaux and the

Water Jousting

One of Languedoc's strangest traditional sports is the water jousting — *joutes nautiques* — at Sète, Agde, and other waterfront towns. The tournaments at Sète during the month of August are the best known. Armed with 3-metre lances and holding shields, two jousters dressed in splendid white costume stand precariously on long projecting platforms (*tintaines*) at the end of decorated rowing boats — one blue and one red — vigorously propelled forward by their ten team mates. Also on board are a pair of musicians, who play the tune of the 300-year-old 'jousting songs', always sung for the occasion, which keep spirits high as the opponents each try to toss the other as ignominiously as possible into the canal.

du Midi; the Sailors' Cemetery (Cimetière Marin) and, finally, the St. Charles Cemetery. It's a stiff climb right to the top of Mont St. Clair, where a chapel, Notre-Dame-de-la-Salette, commands a magnificent view across most of Languedoc and Roussillon from the Cévennes to the Pyrenees. There are two festive pilgrimages to the chapel, which are popularly called *Le Grand 19* ('the Great 19th', on 19th September) and *Le 19 des Vendangeurs* ('the Grape-Harvesters' 19th', on 19th October).

Water jousting at Sète

Overleaf: *The river Hérault at Agde*

Sète in its present form is about 300 years old; the name was always spelt Cette until this century. It has passed the years with little incident, although during the Camisard War (see p. 8) the town was attacked and seized by the English, who intended to give support to the Protestant rebels but were driven back again after just a few days. The town came into being with the Canal du Midi, Pierre-Paul de Riquet's elegant masterpiece of civil engineering, which he designed and constructed between 1666 and 1681. At the same time he also built the network of waterways which comprise the harbour of the town. Riquet himself was born not far away, at Béziers, through which his canal runs, and where his statue now stands.

Sète has had famous sons of its own, and they tended to love their native town with a considerable degree of passion. Best known of them were the accomplished Académie Française poet and scientist Paul Valéry (1871–1945), who declared 'I was born in one of the places where I would love to have been born', and the poetic, political rock-folk singer and friend of Sartre, George Brassens (1921–1981). Valéry is buried in the Cimetière Marin, while Brassens' grave, despite his plea 'to be buried on the beach at Sète', can be seen in the new cemetery which looks out over the Étang de Thau.

On the seashore below the cemeteries, old Vauban defences called the Fort St. Pierre, or lately the Theatre of the Sea, are the scene of an annual Theatre Festival. Beside the fortifications extends the jetty they were built to protect, Môle St. Louis, which separates the town and its harbour from the sea.

Long waves roll slowly onto the straight, windswept Isthme des Onglous, an unbroken 20km ribbon of sand connecting Sète to Agde. Almost no development or dwellings interrupt the beach road (N112) until, just before Agde, it reaches **Marseillan-Plage**, a small modern tourist centre with a number of cheap seashore campsites. The resort is quite without colour or attraction, and is deserted outside the high season, but the beach is good. Just to its west, within walking distance, is Agde's naturist beach, and this can be an easier approach to it than through Cap d'Agde. Just a short drive inland, the real **Marseillan** is an unassuming village of tremendous age. It was probably founded in about 500BC by residents of adjacent Agde or colonists from present-day Marseille, then a Greek city called Massalia (the Romans later changed it to Massilia). At that time, Marseillan was on the seashore, and was principally an outpost of fishermen and farmers, and a stopping point for coastal trading ships plying to or from Agde and Marseille. Nowadays it survives mainly from the surrounding vineyards and manufacturing the apéritif Noilly Prat (caves open to visitors).

Most popular of all Languedoc's resort areas, **Cap d'Agde**, until recently an almost deserted stretch of coast, has been transformed into a cluster of holiday villages attracting over 1½ million visitors each year. The Cap itself is a black volcanic mound with black sand fringes, but extending away in both directions are gorgeous fine golden sand beaches shallowing into the sea. The best of the beaches is the long, wide strand which belongs to the phenomenal Quartier Naturiste. This is a special holiday village — or town, rather — with several shopping centres, semi-circular apartment blocks (in some ways reminiscent of la Grande-Motte), car parks, restaurants, cafés, campsites and, in total, accommodation for some 20,000 visitors. Complete nudity throughout the Quartier Naturiste is the general rule, although it is not obligatory and indeed such a concrete and even urban environment is perhaps not ideal for naturists. However, it is a far-reaching and liberating experience, well worth having, and people who have spent a whole fortnight in the Naturist Quarter (and some visitors spend a month or more) say they are in real danger of venturing out without remembering how to dress properly.

The non-naturist part of Cap d'Agde aimed towards a more traditional style of architecture, tall narrow houses of uneven heights with Roman tile roofs. However, to be honest, the resemblance to a real village is slight. None the less it is a relatively pleasing development. It is large enough to be worth

spending several days exploring, and there is plenty of entertainment for both adults and children. The resort, though largely closed down out of season, does have a permanent population of 3,000.

4km inland, the small town of **Agde** is popular and touristy. Although there is an intriguing old quarter of narrow lanes, it really has remarkably little to show for its long history, which stretches right back to the earliest civilisation of the Languedoc coast. Greek Phocaeans established the seaport of Agathe Tyche (meaning Good Fortune in their language), which was then on the coast at the mouth of the river Hérault (it's the coast which has moved, not Agde) at around 600BC, about the same time that they settled at Massalia (Marseille). From both towns they traded with Greece and the Levant and with each other. By the time the Romans were taking over this part of the world Agathe had become by far the largest port town on the Languedoc coast, and it continued to flourish under their rule. In AD400 it

---

Naturism

The relatively minority interest of naturism (nudity) has become big business for Languedoc. Extensive facilities have been provided at some of the new beach resorts for people who want an all-over tan. Perhaps this is because before the recent development of the coast the area had a reputation for being secluded and unfrequented and was therefore an ideal spot for anyone wanting to strip off. Cap d'Agde's huge and popular 'Quartier Naturiste' now has its own shops, restaurants, accommodation for 20,000, the best of the beaches, and is one of the town's principal sources of income. There's a nudists' area at adjacent la Tamarissière too, while farther down the seashore there are two more naturist 'villages' at Leucate, and another at Fleury d'Aude. All have beaches and good facilities set aside especially for naturists.

became an episcopal capital, and, fighting off various invasions over the centuries, so it remained for an astonishing 1,390 years. By then, though, both Montpellier and Sète had begun to overtake it in importance, and in the 18th century Agde went into rapid decline. In recent years tourism has revived it, giving it more life, more traffic, and lots of crêperies, pizzerias and inexpensive eating places.

Agde used to be called the Ville Noire, the black town, because it was built all of dark volcanic rock from the nearby Mont St Loup. It is not especially black-looking now, not even in the heart of the old quarter, although the grim, dark and heavily fortified cathedral, originally 9th-century, rebuilt in the 12th, restored in the 17th and 19th, is a reminder of how Agde earned its nickname. Agde's cathedral is not even slightly beautiful, and was clearly designed with defence as the top priority. It has some unusual characteristics: sheer walls rising to castellations and a belltower modelled on a keep; inside, the nave at right-angles to the choir, and a handsomely vaulted ceiling.

Behind the cathedral the river Hérault, at last almost within sight of the sea after its journey down from the Cévennes, flows within black embankments towards the beach resort villages of **le Grau-d'Agde** on the left bank and **la Tamarissière** on the right. Traditional water jousting contests, in a boisterous and festive atmosphere, take place on this waterway during the summer.

The Corbières wine village of Fitou

Étangs

One of the most striking features of the Languedoc coastline is the chain of shallow reedy saltwater lakes or lagoons — *étangs* — which lie right behind the beaches. As recently as in Roman times these did not exist, and village or towns on the *étangs'* inland (north or west) sides were in those days right on the seafront. Agde and Marseillan, for example, were seaports. Drifting sand and alluvial deposits from the Rhône were a serious problem for Languedoc's harbours throughout the Middle Ages. Constant dredging was necessary to keep them free of sand and mud. The cost of keeping open the shipping channels at Aigues-Mortes proved prohibitive and the town had to be abandoned altogether in the 14th century. The large port at Narbonne, so important in Greek and Roman times, also became irretrievably silted-up during the 14th century after being left uncleared for fifty years. At this time offshore sandbars were forming which were to create a new coastline, cutting off areas of seawater in the form of inland lakes. They remain full of saltwater because the *étangs* are connected to the sea by narrow channels called *graus*. Old associations with the lagoons were mosquitoes and salt extraction: both have now largely disappeared. Today, the *étangs* are known for oysters, flamingos and rare birds.

There is no proper coast road here; N112, not far inland, goes from Agde towards Béziers (see p. 92). Turnings off the route nationale lead towards beach developments and fishing ports dotted along this stretch of coast, still relatively unknown to tourists. Biggest of them is **Valras-Plage**. Either skirt through the edges of Béziers, or by-pass the town completely by taking little country lanes like the D37ᴱ, to reach **Fleury d'Aude** (8km inland) and its seashore developments. Fleury's new beach resort spreads between **St. Pierre-sur-Mer** and the fishing community of **les Cabanes de Fleury** on the mouth of the river Aude, and is intent upon an 'ecological' image. Its planners describe the layout of beach-side Fleury as presenting 'a deliberately untamed appearance'. Indeed it has adopted such a low profile that, I notice, it is still not being marked even on some of the most recent maps of the area! It has a quiet, family holiday atmosphere, with botanical gardens, woodland paths and picnic areas as well as seaside attractions. Despite the efforts to create a brand new resort centre here, it is older St. Pierre which has become the focus of Fleury's tourism. Les Cabanes has also been transformed by the arrival of holiday-makers, but does retain something of its previous non-touristic atmosphere. Close to St. Pierre there's a grotto — Gouffre de l'Oeil Doux — with an eerie black lake.

A coast road, running beside lovely *garrigue*-covered rocks, connects St. Pierre with its unappealing neighbour **Narbonne-Plage**, which has a long wide sandy beach backed by a string of what the French call *parkings* (car parks), and new resort **Gruissan** which envelops an older fishing village, clustering around a promontory on which stands the ruined 13th-century tower of Barberousse (or Barbarossa). Opinions vary widely about all Languedoc's coastal developments, but certainly the new part of Gruissan would have looked better to my eye if the architects had put ordinary Roman tiles on the roofs instead of quasi-Islamic arches. A curiosity on the flat windswept sands of Gruissan's waterfront is the makeshift cottages built on stilts to protect them from high tides.

Rising behind the coast, the **Montagne de la Clape** (214m) is spectacular, a fascinating rocky terrain penetrated by twisting, confusing narrow lanes with sudden and lovely views of the blue Mediterranean. Small vineyards cover fertile nooks and crannies on the lower slopes, and they produce some of the Coteaux du Languedoc's better wines. This is the area of the La Clape and Quatourze labels. I have often heard it said that Quatourze is one of the oldest vineyard districts in France, but have as yet been unable to find the evidence for this. Whatever their histories, both wines are enjoyable. On one of the two 'summits' of the Montagne de la Clape, gazing pensively down at the sea through a screen of parasol pinewoods, is a Sailors' Cemetery. Both picturesque and terribly sad, it consists of scores of humble memorial stones — no one is buried here, for all the dead were lost at sea — erected among the rocks by families and friends. A rustic little chapel, Notre-Dame des Auzils, stands beside the Cemetery.

Once again, a short diversion inland is necessary, this time via Narbonne (see p. 97), although one simple way to avoid the town is to take a quick trip on the autoroute just as far as the next exit. No road crosses the expanse of seashore *étangs* just here, so take N9 which runs around the back of the lagoons. It passes a popular Safari Park (on the left just before Sigean) and a turning to **Port-la-Nouvelle**, a small waterside town which tries, without much success, to combine being a ghastly industrial port with another persona as a tourist centre with a fine beach. This can be safely by-passed. N9 presses on, skirting *étangs* towards the Roussillon border. On the way it passes the village of **Fitou**, a lovely little wine-making community which has given its name to one of Languedoc's best *Appellations*.

The village lies peacefully just off the road. For those who love Fitou's strong dark red wine, which despite growing popularity is still inexpensive and unaffected but very palatable (I am one of its fans!), it is satisfying to make a stop at this pretty village, even though the real heartland of Fitou *Appellation* lies farther inland (see p. 131). There seems to be a lot of restoration work being done on Fitou's old stone houses, a result perhaps of the villagers' new-found prosperity brought about by charging slightly higher prices for their wine and selling more of it. Climbing flowers draped over some of the doorways give the place charm. The imposing ruin of a hilltop castle overlooks the village. The fascinating little 12th-century parish church is dedicated, most unusually, to a married couple: St. Julien and his wife

Overleaf: *The lighthouse-tower on the waterfront at Collioure*

Ste. Basilisse. The church was originally a dependency of the Abbey of Fontfroide, which owned a good deal of this part of Languedoc. Fitou stands at the edge of the haunting rocky landscapes of the Corbières, which extend away inland from the village. For a brief excursion into this rugged, sunny terrain of *garrigue* and vineyards, follow signs a couple of kilometres towards 'St. Aubin — Pla de Fitou'. These lead eventually along a rough track to a tiny 9th-century Carolingian chapel in beautiful condition. With a roof of stone tiles and a miniature belfry, it stands in the grounds of an isolated little house. To see the intriguing interior of the little chapel just ring at the door of the house and ask. (Entrance is free: offer a tip.)

But instead of rushing straight down on N9, one can stay right on the coast by taking a left turn (D627) to the old village of **Leucate**, with its beachfront at **Leucate-Plage**, a rocky outlook at **Cap Leucate**, and one of the new resorts at **Port-Leucate**. (Note: this turning is shortly *before* Fitou, but it's worth going as far as Fitou just to see the village, and then returning to the Leucate road.) Leucate's old village, dominated by its ruined fortress — for we are almost on the former troubled frontier with Spain — looks out across an *étang*, the northern half of which is called Étang de Leucate, and the southern half Étang de Salses. A stone's throw from the village is peaceful **la Franqui**, facing out to sea across its beach and its pines. A footpath climbs over the Cap and joins it to sedate old Leucate-Plage.

Port-Leucate, perched half-way along a narrow sandbar 8km long, is almost like an island, squeezed between *étang* and Mediterranean, and it has tried not to abandon the relaxed and traditional seaside image of la Franqui and Leucate-Plage. It offers one of the largest marina and leisure ports on this coast, and with many low-level white-painted buildings has succeeded better than some of its rivals in creating a modern but unobtrusive and acceptable life style. Like Agde, it has set out to attract naturists, who have their own campsites here. In some ways Port-Leucate is a rather calm and gentle place, considering that it's a Mediterranean beach resort, and it has managed not to wreak too much havoc on existing communities nor on the watery environment. Port-Leucate extends along the sands to merge indistinguishably with Port-Barcarès. There is one unusual landmark between the two though — a beached liner, the *Lydia*, now transformed into a nightclub, restaurant and casino!

At this point we are leaving Languedoc and entering Catalan-speaking Roussillon: on the other side of the *étang* is the sturdy red-brick Fort de Salses (p. 143) which kept guard over the frontier of the province, once part of Spain (see Chapter 7 — French Catalonia).

Port-Barcarès describes itself as 'vital', and puts the accent on sports, fitness and dynamic leisure activities. Being surrounded by *étang* and sea, obviously watersports dominate, with windsurfing and sailing especially popular because of the constant breezes which blow over this coast ... but there are plenty of facilities for tennis, riding, cycling, golf, gymnastics, body-building, judo, moto-cross, four-wheel drive rallies, volleyball, aero-

Festivals on the Coast

Mi-Carème (usually Thursday of the 3rd Week of Lent, Carème)

MARSEILLAN - lively local fête with traditional music and dance.

Easter

COLLIOURE — Procession des Pénitents: colourful Good Friday procession of hooded Black Penitents through the old quarter and to the waterfront church.

Sunday nearest 29th June

SÈTE — Grand Pardon de St. Pierre; traditional processions and water jousting.
AGDE, PALAVAS and VALRAS — Fête de la St. Pierre (or Fête des Pêcheurs): local festivals of the sea.

August

SÈTE — Théâtre de la Mer: open-air waterside theatre performances all month.
PALAVAS — Fête de la Mer (on 14th): festivities and water jousting.
FRONTIGNAN — (13th–21st): water jousting, traditional entertainments, bullfights.
SÈTE — Fête de St. Louis (Monday nearest 25th): more processions and water jousting for the town's patron saint.

September, October

SÈTE — 1st Sun in September: floodlit nocturnal water jousting.
SÈTE — Festive pilgrimages to the chapel at the summit of Mont St. Clair overlooking the town on 19th September (Le Grand 19) and 19th October (Le 19 des Vendangeurs).

bics, dancing, archery and just about everything else! Port-Barcarès also specialises in what the spa-loving French call Thalassothérapie, health treatments using seawater baths.

The coast road (D81) passes undeveloped villages on the seashore or just inland. Perpignan (p. 145) is not far away, and modern **Canet-Plage** is the favourite weekend or day-out resort area for the city. A wide sandy beach and plenty of entertainment facilities, including a famous toy museum called the Musée du Père Noël, Father Christmas Museum, ensure that it is crowded most of the year. The museum houses over 4,000 unusual and historic toys and games (some dating back to Sumerian times) donated to the mayor of Canet by a personal friend, Jean-Claude Baudot, a prosperous local viticulteur who has become the world's leading expert on the Santa Claus myth.

9km of sandy beach, backed by a road and an *étang*, connect Canet to **St. Cyprien-Plage** ('St. Cyp' to its friends), the farthest south of the new resorts. Another lively, sporty holiday town of characterless new buildings, St. Cyp is redeemed by plenty of green space, the backdrop of the Pyrenees, the old Catalan village of St. Cyprien just inland, and a balmy southern climate.

Although St. Cyp is the most southerly of the built-from-scratch new developments, **Argelès-Plage**, even farther down the coast, had a lot of money pumped in to transform it from an uninspiring seaside village to a modern holiday resort specialising in low-cost accommodation, especially camping. It has a grand total of 62 campsites (over 13,000 places) in the 2- to 4-star categories. Just inland, on the fringes of the Albères range of Pyrenean foothills, the village of **Argelès-sur-Mer** retains parts of its old ramparts and medieval centre. The old quarter is dominated by a fortified square tower, and there is a small Catalan museum. In Roman times, as its name suggests, this older community was itself on the seashore.

The coast south of here is called the **Côte Vermeille**, undoubtedly the most beautiful part of the Languedoc–Roussillon seashore. For this is where the Pyrenees actually touch the Mediterranean, tumbling down into the exquisite blue water to create gorgeous coves and sandy bays backed by high rocky slopes. The coast road clings to the mountainsides on *corniches* with dazzling sea views. The word Vermeille defies ready translation into

English. It comes from Vermeil, which means both vermilion and silver gilt. The ruddy rock colour and brilliant morning sunshine, and in autumn the hillsides draped in red vine leaves, do give this stretch of coast a bright rose-tinted appearance. The vine is all-important on these sunny sea-facing hills. From them come the best of Roussillon's heady wines, especially the distinctive rich sweet reds which carry the Banyuls *Appellation*.

From Argelès the road (N114) twists for a half-dozen kilometres to enter the jewel of the Côte Vermeille, **Collioure**. This Catalan fishing village has for centuries been impressing travellers and traders, artists and invaders, with its simple beauty. It consists of a perfect little gem of a harbour, protected by sea walls and a fortified 14th-century village church on one side and a mighty 12th-century 'Royal Castle' on the other. Looking down from an adjacent summit the 15th-century Fort Miradou, still an army barracks, provides additional protection for the tiny but strategic port. Beside the church, with its curious round light-house-tower (and inside, superb Baroque altarpieces), small beaches bask tranquilly in the sun or catch the sea winds according to the day's weather. From the heights of the château — in fact a modest castle of the Majorcan kings enclosed by massive French fortifications — the red and yellow stripes of the Catalan flag flutter in the southern breeze. Behind the harbourfront is a delightful tangle of picturesque narrow lanes and alleys alive with atmosphere and history. Here local people shop and stroll and live their lives almost oblivious of the foreign visitors. Indeed, only a few visitors ever venture into the village, preferring — and who can blame them — to sit at the open-air café and restaurant tables, shaded under big awnings, along the pleasant waterfront. Fish dishes are, not surprisingly, a great speciality here; above all Collioure is noted for excellent anchovies.

Among the harbourside establishments, the popular and rather unkempt Hôtel les Templiers makes the most extraordinary and marvellous place to stay. I have found, in common with many before, that the staff attitude to customers leaves something to be desired; but it's all worth it to stay in this veritable art gallery of a hotel, the walls of which are crammed with hundreds of original paintings and signed prints and posters left behind by the illustrious and less illustrious artists who used to patronise it regularly: Picasso, Derain, Matisse, Braque, and many others. A virtual garret on the top floor, my own room at the hotel looked across the jumble of adjacent red-tile rooftops, big French windows opened wide to let in the gentle, temperate air, while hanging on the room's plain white wall was a sunny Impressionist painting left in payment by a former guest.

On the other side of the 'Château Royal' there's another good beach and smaller harbour, and latter-day Collioure has spread round to provide this stretch of shore with its own cafés and restaurants which are cheaper than in the old village.

Next town along the coast is **Port-Vendres**, administrative centre of the Côte Vermeille district, a bright and lively harbour with a few expensive-looking yachts moored among many humbler working vessels. This was the Romans' Portus-Veneris, the Port of Venus (or Gate of Venus if the name was really Porta Veneris as some claim), and has prospered gently ever since. The harbour was fortified by Vauban, but has a modern appearance having been largely rebuilt following bomb damage in 1944.

Between Port-Vendres and Banyuls, lovely vine-coloured hills descend to gorgeous blue rocky bays. Rising and falling through the rolling vineyards of the Banyuls *Appellation*, the road soon reaches **Banyuls** itself. Behind the agreeable waterfront with its palm and eucalyptus trees and café tables, there's an older area of narrow lanes and steps intertwined with shady newer streets. The town was a centre of the Templars, and their wine cellars survive and can be visited. Banyuls (pronounce the 's') has long been noted for its intriguing wines, especially a sweet port-like red, and the strong Vieux Banyuls. There are numerous opportunities for *dégustatation*, tasting.

The sculptor Aristide Maillol (1861–1944) was born at Banyuls, and is buried in a rustic spot 4km inland at the Métairie Maillol. Another interior back-road (D86 — Route du Balcon de Madeloc) returns from here through beautiful high country to Collioure, passing the lofty Madeloc tower (14th century). While on the coast, N114 clings to the high waterside cliffs for the 10km to the last village in France, **Cerbère**. Despite the rather sinister name (i.e. Cerberus, the monstrous dog which guarded the gate of Hell in Classical mythology!), Cerbère is a popular little resort in a plunging bay enclosed by mountains.

Hotels and Restaurants

AGDE and CAP D'AGDE:
La Tamarissière, 21 quai Théophile-Cornu (67.94.20.87), pleasant riverside hotel and excellent restaurant specialising in local seafood dishes, good value.
La Brasero, Port-Richelieu II, at the Cap (67.26.24.75), lively bistro with good food at moderate prices.
Les Trois Sergents, av des Sergents (67.26.73.13), a large Art Deco restaurant with fine cooking at reasonable prices.
Hôtel Ève, at the Cap (67.26.71.70), completely naturist hotel, modern, rather expensive.
Note also, **Hôtel Léonce**, excellent restaurant and modest Logis at FLORENSAC, just inland from Agde.

ARGELÈS-SUR-MER:
Le Lido, 50 bd de la Mer (68.81.10.32), straightforward modern hotel–restaurant beside sea.
Hôtel–Restaurant Le Cottage, 21 rue Arthur-Rimbaud (68.81.07.33), modest little 2-star Logis, inexpensive.

BANYULS-SUR-MER:
Hôtel–Restaurant Les Elmes, Plage des Elmes (68.88.03.12), acceptable little seashore Logis with good, low-priced restaurant.
Restaurant Le Sardinal, pl Paul-Reig (68.88.30.07), fine Catalan cuisine and best of the local wines.

COLLIOURE:
Hôtel–Restaurant Les Templiers, quai de l'Amirauté (68.82.05.58), popular quayside restaurant–bar–hotel, full of character, walls covered with original pictures and signed prints, acceptable prices. See p. 191.
Hôtel–Restaurant La Frégate, 24 quai de l'Amirauté (68.82.06.05), reasonable quayside hotel with good seafood restaurant.
Casa Pairal, impasse des Palmiers (68.82.05.81), lovely town-centre hotel, not cheap.

LA GRANDE-MOTTE: Restaurant Alexandre-Amirauté, Esplanade de la Capitainerie (67.56.63.63), excellent restaurant with regional food and wine, reasonably priced.

GRUISSAN: Le Chebek, quai d'Honneur et du Levant (68.49.02.58), better than average restaurant along this stretch of coast, with good selection of dishes at an acceptable price.

PALAVAS-LES-FLOTS: La Maison de l'Huître, 3 av Foch (67.68.09.85), best restaurant in town, seafood specialities, modest prices.

PORT-VENDRES: Le Chalut, 8 quai François-Joly (68.82.00.91), good little fish and seafood restaurant with local wines, reasonable prices.

SÈTE: **Grand Hôtel**, quai de Lattre-de-Tassigny (67.74.71.77), imposing modernised canalside Logis with good restaurant (**La Rotonde**), not expensive. Good, moderately-priced quayside restaurants: **La Palangrotte** (67.74.80.35); **La Rascasse** (67.74.38.46); **La Rotonde** (67.74.71.77).

Hotel Bookings Service

Loisir-Acceuil: AUDE — 70 rue Aimé-Ramon, 11001 Carcassonne (68.47.09.06).

Museums

AGDE: **Musée 'Escolo dau Sarret'**: rue de la Fraternité (67.94.82.51). Local archaeology and artefacts. *10–12, 2–6. Closed Tue.*
Musée d'Archéologie Sous-Marine et Subaquatique: at La Clape (67.26.81.00). Interesting collection of finds — many Roman and earlier — made by local diving club GRASPA. *15th May–15th Sep: 10–12, 3–10; rest of year: 9–12, 3–6. Closed Mon.*

ARGELÈS-SUR-MER: **Casa Catalana des Albères (Musée d'Arts et Traditions Populaires)**: 4 pl Castellans (68.81.42.74). *Jun–Sep: daily (exc Sun) 9–12, 3–6; Oct–May: daily (exc Sat & Sun) 9.30–12, 3.30–6.*

BANYULS: **Caves des Templiers:** rte du Balcon de Madeloc. Former wine cellars of Knights Templar, audiovisual display. *Jun–Sep: 9–7, rest of year: 9–12, 2–6.*

CANET-PLAGE: **Musée du Père-Noël**: pl Mediterranée (68.80.34.07). Large toy collection with some interesting historic items. *15th Jun–15th Sep: 11am–11pm (exc. Sun: 10–12, 3–6.30); rest of year: 9–12, 3–6.30. Closed Tue.*
Musée de la Voiture Ancienne (68.73.20.29). Vintage cars. *Weekdays: 10–12, 2–6; weekends: 10–12, 2.30–6.30. Fêtes same as weekends.*

COLLIOURE: **'Château Royal'** (68.82.06.43). Summer residence of Majorcan kings, now within 17th-century citadel, also with Catalan folk museum. *Open most days from 23rd Jun–30th Sep: 2.30–7.30pm only.*
Musée de Peinture: rte de Port-Vendres (68.82.11.03). Fine art collection. *Jun–Sep, 3–7pm only.*

FRONTIGNAN: **Musée de Frontignan**: 3bis rue Lucien Salette (67.48.25.25). Local arts, crafts and archaeological finds. *10–12, 2.30–7. Closed Sun and Mon.*

MAGUELONE: *the former* **cathedral** *is open 9.30–11.30, 3–6.*

ST. CYPRIEN: **Fondation François et Souza Desnoyer:** rue Émile-Zola (68.21.06.96). Paintings by F. Desnoyer and disciples. *Jul–Aug: 3–7; rest of year 2–6. Closed Tue.*

Musée des Artistes Catalans: in Maison Bernard, rue Jules Romain (68.21.32.07). Works by Catalan artists. *Jul–Aug: 3–7; rest of year 2–6. Closed Tue.*

SÈTE: **Musée Paul Valéry:** rue François Desnoyer (67.46.20.98). Surprising collection of fine art, local history and culture, with sections devoted to Paul Valéry and Georges Brassens. *Jul–Aug: 10–12, 2–7; rest of year: 10–12, 2–6. Closed Tues and fêtes.*

Tourist Offices

CRT office (regional information): 12 rue Foch, 34000 Montpellier (67.60.55.42).

Syndicat Mixte pour l'Aménagement Touristique du Languedoc–Roussillon (resort information): 1 rue Maguelonne, 34000 Montpellier (67.92.61.10).

CDT offices (information on the département): AUDE — 39 bd Barbès, 11012 Carcassonne (68.71.30.09); HÉRAULT — pl Gaudechot, 34000 Montpellier (67.54.20.66); PYRENÉES-ORIENTALES — Palais Consulaire, quai de Lattre-de-Tassigny, 66005 Perpignan (68.34.29.94).

OTSI offices (local information): AGDE — rue L. Bages (67.94.29.68); ARGELÈS-SUR-MER — pl des Arènes (68.81.15.85); BANYULS-SUR-MER — Hôtel de Ville (68.88.31.58); CANET-PLAGE — pl de la Méditerranée (68.80.20.65); CERBÈRE — 1 av de la Côte Vermeille (68.88.42.36); COLLIOURE — quai de l'Amirauté (68.82.15.47); LA GRANDE-MOTTE — pl du 1er-Octobre (67.56.62.62); GRUISSAN — bd Pech-Meynaud (68.49.03.25); LEUCATE — call 68.40.91.31 for information; PALAVAS-LES-FLOTS — Hôtel de Ville (67.68.02.34); PORT-BARCARÈS — on seafront (68.86.16.56, 68.86.10.50, 68.86.18.23); PORT-VENDRES — quai Forgas (68.82.07.54); ST. CYPRIEN-PLAGE — quai A. Rimbaud (68.21.01.33) or quai de la Pêche (68.21.08.14); SÈTE — 22 quai d'Alger (67.74.73.00), sometimes also pl A. Briand (67.74.05.86).

Where there is no tourist office, apply to the Town Hall (Mairie or Hôtel de Ville).

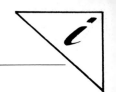

Sports and Leisure

Contact Syndicats d'Initiative in each town for useful addresses and phone numbers. Most resorts have other activities in addition to the following:

ARCHERY — Agde (67.94.08.14), Port-Barcarès (68.86.12.37); CLAY-PIGEON SHOOTING — Agde (67.94.92.97); DIVING — la Grande-Motte (Centre Nautique 67.56.62.64), Collioure (68.82.06.34), Argelès (68.81.16.33), Banyuls (68.38.31.66); GOLF — la Grande-Motte (85-hectare course, 67.56.05.00), St. Cyprien (68.21.01.71); PARASCENDING — la Grande-Motte (Centre Nautique 67.56.62.64), Agde (on Plage de la Roquille), Banyuls (68.88.33.43); RIDING — Agde (67.21.26.99), Port-Barcarès (68.86.07.82), St. Cyprien (68.21.18.10); SAILING — la Grande-Motte (Centre Nautique 67.56.62.64), Agde (Centre Nautique 67.26.81.93), Leucate (68.40.91.31), Port-Barcarès (Centre Nautique 68.86.07.28); TENNIS — la Grande Motte (34 courts, 67.56.62.63), Agde (62 courts, 67.26.00.06), Leucate (24 courts, 68.40.98.85), Port-Barcarès (27 courts, 68.86.06.83), St. Cyprien (17 courts, 68.21.24.21), Gruissan (16 courts, 68.49.24.25); Argelès (11 courts, 68.81.33.29); THALASSOTHÉRAPY (seawater spa) — Agde (67.26.14.80), la Grande-Motte (67.85.01.13), Port-Barcarès (68.86.30.90); WIND-SURFING — la Grande-Motte (Centre Nautique 67.56.62.64), Agde (Centre Nautique 67.26.81.93), Port-Barcarès (Centre Nautique 68.86.07.28); WATER-SKIING — la Grande-Motte (Centre Nautique 67.56.62.64), Agde (Plage de la Roquille), Leucate (68.40.91.31), Port-Barcarès (Centre Nautique 68.86.07.28).

Theme Parks and Activities for Children

AQUALAND, Agde — 30 hectares of water amusements (all at constant 25°C) for adults and children, waterslides, wave pools, 'funny rapids', children's pools, shops and restaurants (67.26.71.09); closed out of season.
AGDE — children's sports clubs, riding, go-karting, roller-skating, etc.
LEUCATE — children's beachclubs, swimming lessons, volleyball and tennis coaching, waterski and sailing courses, etc.
ST. CYPRIEN — children's beachclubs, go-karting, tuition in tennis and football.

Index

Notes: *Saint* comes before *Sainte* — eg *St Sernin-sur-Rance* before *Ste Énimie*: place names beginning with *le* or *la* are listed by the initial of the following word — eg *le Boulou*, *le Vigan*, etc

196